Choices, Chances and Changes - Doing Business in Ghana

Choices, Chances and Changes - Doing Business in Ghana

Richard Boateng

Choices, Chances and Changes – Doing Business in Ghana
Part of the Cases for Academic Study Series – Volume 1

All rights reserved. No part of this *publication* may be reproduced, distributed, or transmitted in any form or by any means, including photocopying, recording, or other electronic or mechanical methods, without the prior written permission of the publisher, except in the case of *brief quotations* embodied in critical reviews and certain other noncommercial uses permitted by copyright law. For permission requests, write to the publisher at the address below.

Edited By:
RICHARD **BOATENG**
Email: richard@pearlrichards.org

Copyright © 2016 Richard Boateng

CreateSpace Independent Publishing Platform
Charleston, USA.
eStore address (i.e. www.CreateSpace.com/6657374)
Printed by CreateSpace, An Amazon.com Company
CreateSpace, Charleston SC

ISBN: 1539626296
ISBN 13: 9781539626299

To God Be The Glory
Just By Your Grace

To My Wife and Daughter
You Mean The World To Me

Table of Contents

LIST OF EXHIBITS · xi

PREFACE AND ACKNOWLEDGMENTS · xiii

CONTRIBUTORS · 1

TEACHING AND LEARNING WITH CASE STUDIES · 3
    CASE STUDY DEFINED · 3
    BENEFITS AND IMPORTANCE OF CASE STUDIES · 4
    HOW TO ANALYSE CASE STUDIES · 4

MAPPING THE CASE STUDIES WITH TOPICS IN BUSINESS AND
MANAGEMENT STUDIES · 8

HOW GHANAIAN MOBILE SERVICE PROVIDERS CREATE SERVICES · · · · · · · · · 10
    FIRM HISTORY AND PROFILE · 10
    NANDIMOBILE M-BUSINESS SERVICES · 13
    A LEARNING EXPERIENCE · 16
    FINDING NEW RESOURCES AND RETIRING CAPABILITIES · · · · · · · · · · · · · · · · 19
    DEVELOPING NEW RESOURCES · 20
    RESOURCE RECONFIGURATION · 25
    CHALLENGES · 25
    CURRENT AND FUTURE PROJECTS · 27
    QUESTIONS · 31

HIS PRESENCE HOTEL LIMITED: APPRECIATING PEOPLE AND ACTING RESPONSIBLY ... 32
History and Company Profile ... 32
Organizational Culture and HRM Practices ... 34
Industry's Recognition of Corporate Social Responsibility (CSR) ... 36
Classification of social responsibility ... 38
A Look Toward the Future ... 40
Questions ... 42

CRM IMPLEMENTATION IN A GHANAIAN REAL ESTATE COMPANY ... 45
Firm Profile ... 45
Background to the CRM Implementation ... 46
Reasons behind the Adoption of CRM ... 47
Features of the Sales Information Management Systems (SIMS) ... 48
Implementation Challenges ... 49
Efforts at Addressing the Challenges ... 51
Benefits of the CRM system ... 52
Questions ... 54

UNIVERSITY OF GHANA ACCESS CONTROL PROJECT ... 56
Problem Context ... 56
Development and Implementation of UG Access Control System ... 59
Factors which shaped the Project ... 63
Discussion and Conclusion ... 65
Questions ... 66

BANK CUSTOMER SERVICE CONCERNS IN BF BANK OF GHANA ... 69
Firm Information ... 69
Recent Innovations ... 70
Questions ... 74

DEVELOPING E-COMMERCE CAPABILITIES IN A BEVERAGE MANUFACTURING FIRM ... 75
Kasadrin Company Limited - Firm Profile ... 75
Business Resource Development ... 78
E-commerce Capabilities Development ... 83

MANAGING RESOURCES TO ADDRESS CONSTRAINTS 91
IMPACT OF E-COMMERCE ACTIVITIES 94
QUESTIONS 94

FACTORS WHICH INFLUENCE MOBILE BANKING ADOPTION 96
PROFILE OF ABC BANK GHANA LIMITED 96
THEORETICAL LENS: TECHNOLOGY ORGANIZATION ENVIRONMENT (TOE) MODEL · 96
RESEARCH QUESTIONS 101

ENHANCING LIVELIHOODS THROUGH MOBILE BUSINESS 102
BACKGROUND INFORMATION 102
CURRENT BUSINESS INFORMATION AND START-UP STORY 103
OPERATIONAL ISSUES 104
VULNERABILITY, THREATS AND CHALLENGES 106
QUESTIONS 107

USING THEORIES TO ANALYZE CASE STUDIES 108
DEFINING THEORY 108
RESOURCE-BASED THEORY (RBT) AND DYNAMIC CAPABILITIES (DC) FRAMEWORK 109

List of Exhibits

Exhibit 1 Sample Institutions using NandiMobile's Products	11
Exhibit 2 NandiMobile's Financial Profile	12
Exhibit 3 The Process of Subscribing to a NandiMobile Service	21
Exhibit 4 Sample FC Advert with Keyword and Short Code	23
Exhibit 5 Sample Response from Texting FC's Keyword to 1945	23
Exhibit 6 First Capital Plus' *Speedbanking* m-Service	29
Exhibit 7 Financial Profile of Kasadrin Company Limited	77
Exhibit 8 Homepage of the www.kasadringh.com (flash version)	86
Exhibit 9 Mobile Kiosk of Abubakari Sulley	103

Preface and Acknowledgments

You are welcome to Choices, Chances and Changes – Doing Business in Ghana. This book is part of the Cases for Academic Study Series – Volume 1. I put this book together as a guide for faculty and students seeking to explore theoretical concepts through real world case studies. It is also a companion for the application of case studies in the teaching of topics in business and management, thus bridging the gap between theory and practice.

This book aims to be a practice-based teaching material on mobile business, marketing, corporate social responsibility, mobile health, entrepreneurship, electronic commerce/business, and technology entrepreneurship in higher educational institutions. The case studies are drawn from existing companies in Ghana in order to provide students an opportunity to explore and learn from the Choices, Chances and Changes experienced by these companies. These companies are in different stages of their growth. The case studies explore the real problems that micro-entrepreneurs, small and medium enterprises and public institutions face or have to address such as opportunity recognition, differentiation, access to markets, managing customers and lack of capital.

The appropriate use of these case studies in teaching will facilitate the application of theories and concepts in management and business studies. It will also encourage active learning, enhance understanding of industry and practice and lead to the development of skills in communication, collaboration, team work and problem solving. The book also features an overview of two strategic management theories, which can be used to analyze the case studies.

Thanks go to all the contributors of the different case studies in the book. After eight years of compiling these cases, the first edition of the book is out. I am very grateful for your support.

Last but definitely not least, many thanks to my wife, Sheena Lovia Boateng, for her understanding, motivation and support. She is the inspiration for my writing and my life. Because of her, as wife, supporter, and detailed and careful editor, this work has been made possible. To our daughter, Astrid, Mum and Dad say, we love you!

Contributors

Richard Boateng is a technology researcher who focuses on developing concepts into sustainable projects of commercial value and development impact. Richard is an Associate Professor of Information Systems and the Head of the Department of Operations and Management Information Systems at the University of Ghana Business School (UGBS). He can be reached via richboateng@ug.edu.gh

Sheena Lovia Boateng is a marketing consultant and the Director of programmes and events for the PearlRichards Foundation. She is also a marketing PhD candidate in the University of Ghana Business School. Her research interests include relationship marketing, digital marketing, fashion marketing, marketing in micro and small businesses, corporate social responsibility and electronic learning. She can be reached via lovia@pearlrichards.org

Joseph Budu is a lecturer at the School of Technology, Ghana Institute of Management and Policy Administration. He is also a research associate at PearlRichards Foundation. His research interests include mobile business, electronic commerce, design science, and ICT for Development. He can be reached via buduson@gmail.com

Dasmon Alex Akpabli is the founder and CEO of the Daasco Group of Companies. He studied International Business at Fox Business School, Temple University, USA, and Entrepreneurial Management at University of Ghana Business School. He is currently a PhD candidate at UGBS. He can be reached via aakpabli@gmail.com

Kwamena Minta Nyarku is a senior lecturer at the Department of Marketing and Supply Chain Management, School of Business, University of Cape Coast, Ghana. He is also a PhD candidate at the University of Ghana Business School, Legon, Ghana.

Gladys Nkrumah is a lecturer at the Ghana Technology University College. She has a master's degree in Public Administration, and B.Ed in Social Studies. She is currently a PhD Candidate at the University of Ghana Business School. She can be reached via ganny_772000@yahoo.com

Gordon Kofi Sarfo-Adu is a Business Planning Manager at The Forestry Commission (Ghana) in charge of Developing Policies, Programmes, Projects and Business Plans. He holds an MBA in Strategic and Project Management from Paris Graduate School of Management, France, and an MSc in International Accounting and Finance from Buckinghamshire New University, UK. He is currently a PhD candidate at UGBS. He can be reached via gsarfoadu@gmail.com

Emmanuel Oware is an experienced IT practitioner, currently pursuing a PhD in Information Systems at the University of Ghana, Legon. He holds an MBA (Management Information Systems) and a B.Sc in Electrical/ Electronic Engineering. His research interests are in e-Government and systems development and implementation. He can be reached via eoware@aeoptionsgh.com

Ibn Kailan Abdul-Hamid is a PhD Student with the Department of Marketing and Entrepreneurship of the University of Ghana Business School. His research interests are Customer Service; Market Orientation; Firm Positioning; Corporate Social Responsibility; Export Promotion; and Contemporary Marketing Practices. He can be reached via ibnkailan@gmail.com

Nana Yaa Sika Ofori is a Procurement Assistant at ENI Ghana Exploration & Production. She holds an MBA in Management Information Systems from University of Ghana. Her research interests are mobile banking and electronic procurement. She can be reached via nysika88@gmail.com

Desmond Ateh Larkai is a research assistant in the Department of Operations and Management Information Systems at the University of Ghana Business School and a marketing executive at Andcorp Ghana. He currently holds a first class honors Bsc. Administration degree in Electronic Commerce and Customer Management. His research areas are E-Commerce, Customer Relation Marketing and Mobile Technology. He can be reached on deunilark@gmail.com.

Naa Odoley Yehowadah Oddoye is a research assistant in the Department of Operations and Management Information Systems of the University of Ghana Business School. Her research interests are Consumer Behavior, E-Commerce and Mobile Technology. She has completed a B.Sc course in Business Administration (E-Commerce and Customer management option). She can be reached via noyoddoye@st.ug.edu.gh.

Teaching and Learning with Case Studies

Richard Boateng and Sheena Lovia Boateng

Case Study Defined

A case study is an account of an activity or event, and a series of problems, challenges or issues, that contain a real or hypothetical situation which needs to be investigated and solved. They take into account the complexities one would ideally encounter in some contemporary settings, usually but not exclusively an organization (or a person or persons in an organization), by approximating real-world situations (Ellet, 2007; Mauffette-Leenders *et al.*, 2007). Thereby, adding an element of reality to academic studies and helping students to see how these complexities of real life influence decision making. Case studies are essentially used to describe a particularly interesting set of circumstances, from which lessons can be drawn for decision-making. These lessons may also illustrate a particular theory or conceptual framework in academic literature by referencing a specific example; and describing a rare phenomenon or very unusual organization.

They are used to evaluate how well students have understood the relevant theories and concepts, by their ability to apply them to solve the problems posed in the case study. Case studies are usually taken from real life (although true identities are often concealed); they are believable to the reader and include sufficient information for the reader to appreciate the problems and issues. Hence, students are required to analyze academic cases by practicing the application of their intelligence and thinking skills in real situations. They are expected to analyze, apply knowledge, reason and draw effective conclusions, in order to learn from a case study analysis. Good cases for academic studies usually have:

1. A question or problem that needs to be solved.
2. A description of the problem's context
3. Supporting data, which include data tables, links to URLs, quoted statements from case participants, supporting documents, images, video, and audio.

Benefits and Importance of Case Studies

In order to learn a new skill, one needs to practice it continuously. As opposed to the lecturing method, where the instructor tutors and students listen and take notes. In the case study method, students teach themselves, with the instructor merely acting as a guide. Case studies allow students to engage in the practice of strategic management skills by putting themselves figuratively in the decision maker's position. It forces them to tackle business scenarios facing actual managers in the workplace here and now, making it a powerful tool of analysis in academia. Case studies provide students with an active learning experience and varied learning prospects including:

1. Deepening students' understanding of theories as they relate them to practical situations;
2. Helping students to develop a better appreciation of the complexity of problems that may arise in practice and propose applicable solutions to them;
3. Creating analysis, evaluation and decision making skills among students;
4. Teaching students to express ideas in a more concise manner, with clarity;
5. Teaching students to create convincing and well thought arguments; and
6. Motivating and empowering individual students.

How to Analyse Case studies
Step 1: Get a General Impression
Read through the case study without stopping to analyse it. This is to enable you to get a basic understanding of what happened, who is involved and what the general problems are. After, read it a second time to identify the key elements including what

happened; the sequence of events; who was involved; any significant relationships; the facts, as well as the problems. What are your initial impressions of the main issues? Is there a particular strategic issue which the case is oriented towards? Is there any information in the table presented as tables and annexes?

Step 2: Start to Analyze Seriously
With an understanding of the task you have been asked to do, i.e. the assignment question, re-read the case study. This time, clarifying the key issues and identifying the problems which need to be solved, since there will be several different factors at play. Decide which one is the main concern of the case study by examining the main problems raised and the conclusions at the end of the study. One must bear in mind that case studies are written such that students can propose alternative solutions. This is similar to real-life situations where there are usually multiple ways of solving any problem.

Step 3: Develop and Evaluate Strategic Options
Build up a picture of the relative strengths, weaknesses, opportunities and threats (SWOT) for the case in question. Suggest alternative or improved measures that could have been taken by the business. Make use of the information you gathered from the case to trace a sequential progression of steps taken or those not taken, to support your arguments. Integrate the problems using an analysis of theories and concepts learned from previous readings. Evaluate the problems by expressing your opinions, and where applicable, the opinions of other experts; remembering to consider both the benefits and drawbacks of each solution. *Clearly* state what your recommendations are, and justify your choices.

Step 4: Conclude Analysis
Conclude your analysis by reviewing your findings and emphasizing what you would do differently in the case. Write a conclusion that showcases your understanding of the case study, your business strategy, as well as your overall thoughts on the case, as presented in Step 3.

Step 5: Writing Up
Present your response to the case study in the form of a report (depending on the requirements of the assignment given). Diverse instructors will require different formats for case reports. Nonetheless, they all have roughly the same general format.

1. Title page
2. Table of contents
3. Executive summary
4. Problem (Issue) statement
5. Case analysis
6. Key Decision Criteria
7. Analysis of alternatives
8. Recommendations
9. Exhibits

Using Case studies in a Classroom

Extract from Boston University's Centre for Teaching and Learning

In order to start the discussion in class, the instructor can start with an easy, noncontroversial question that all the students should be able to answer readily. However, some of the best case discussions start by forcing the students to take a stand. Some instructors will ask a student to do a formal 'open' of the case, outlining his or her entire analysis. Others may choose to guide discussion with questions that move students from problem identification to solutions. A skilled instructor steers questions and discussion to keep the class on track and moving at a reasonable pace.

In order to motivate the students to complete the assignment before class as well as to stimulate attentiveness during the class, the instructor should grade the participation—quantity and especially quality—during the discussion of the case. This might be a simple check, check-plus, check-minus or zero. The instructor should involve as many students as possible. In order to engage all the students, the instructor can divide them into groups, give each group several minutes to discuss how to answer a question related to the case, and then ask a randomly selected person in each group to present the group's answer and reasoning. Random selection can be accomplished through rolling of dice, shuffled index cards, each with one student's name, a spinning wheel, etc.

http://www.bu.edu/ctl/teaching-resources/using-case-studies-to-teach/

References

Ellet, W. (2007). *The Case Study Handbook: How to Read, Discuss, and Write Persuasively About Cases*, Harvard Business Press.

Mauffette Leenders, L.A., Erskine, J.A. and Leenders, M.R.(2007). *Learning with Cases*, Ivey Publishing.

Mapping the Case Studies with Topics in Business and Management Studies

The case studies documented in this book are relevant for aiding the teaching of the following topics in business and management studies.

How Ghanaian Mobile Service Providers Create Services
- Mobile Business Benefits, Capability Development, Start-up Marketing Strategy, Business Strategy, Managing Competition, Customer management, and Technology Deployment

His Presence Hotel Limited: Appreciating People and Acting Responsibly
- Corporate Social Responsibility, Employee Motivation and Human Resource Management

CRM Implementation in a Ghanaian Real Estate Company
- Customer Relationship Management and Technology Deployment

University of Ghana Access Control Project
- Technology Deployment, Stakeholder Management, Corporate Governance, and Top Management Commitment

Bank Customer Service Concerns in BF Bank of Ghana
- Customer Service and Relationship Management

Enhancing Livelihoods through Mobile Business
- Mobiles for Development, Opportunity Recognition, Mobile Business, and Business Start-up

Developing E-Commerce Capabilities in a Beverage Manufacturing Firm
- Electronic Business or Electronic Commerce Benefits, Capability Development, Business Start-up, Marketing Strategy, Business Strategy, Managing Competition, Technology Deployment, Managing Competition, and Outsourcing

Factors which Influence Mobile Banking Adoption
- Opportunity Recognition, Business Strategy, Technology Deployment and Mobile Banking Challenges.

How Ghanaian Mobile Service Providers Create Services

Joseph Budu and Richard Boateng

> This case study explores the strategic efforts of a mobile service provider in orienting its resources to develop capabilities which create value in the mobile business industry in Ghana.

Firm History and Profile

Nandimobile is a product of the Meltwater Entrepreneurial School of Technology's (MEST) two-year training programme. The MEST programme is a fully sponsored trainee program for young tertiary graduates with a focus on software development and entrepreneurship (Meltwater, 2012). MEST supports trainees to create their own software companies and thereby creating wealth locally in Ghana. Every year, MEST recruits trainees with diverse academic backgrounds like computer science, engineering, business and other social sciences. MEST takes them through a rigorous, two-year training program, after which trainees with viable business ideas move into the MEST Incubator for assistance in getting their businesses off the ground. The Meltwater Foundation and its networks of experienced mentors and advisors also provide mentorship for the companies that make it out of the incubator (Meltwater, 2012).

Anne Amuzu, Edward Tagoe, and Michael Dakwa, co-founders of Nandimobile graduated from MEST in May/June 2010, and are currently housed in the Incubator in East Legon, Accra. The three co-founders hold first degrees in Computer Engineering,

Psychology and Building Technology, respectively. The Nandimobile team received funding after MEST adjudged Gripeline (their flagship product) as viable, and replicable across countries. After the acceptance, Anne and her mates formed Nandimobile, incorporated on 26 June 2010. They received an undisclosed initial amount from MEST. According to MEST, the funding normally between $30,000 and $300,000 is for a minority equity stake in start-ups like Nandimobile, and also to enable the new companies to produce a commercially viable solution and generate initial revenue. Other facilities provided for start-ups include office space, access to a network of advisors/mentors, and hands-on assistance in the business aspects from incubator staff. Nandimobile, a *Value Added Service Provider*, clocked its third year in June 2013. Having started with three (3) core members, the company now has a staff strength of eight (8). This number includes Anne, the Chief Executive Officer, Edward, the Business Development Manager, and Michael, the Technical Manager. Others are Joseph, a mobile applications developer who reports to Michael; and two Sales Team Managers, Selorm and Belinda who report to Edward. Each Sales Team Manager also has one Sales Officer. Whilst Selorm holds a first degree in Marketing, Berlinda holds a first degree in Human Biology, with a passion for sales.

Several businesses from various industries like automobile, body care and beauty, and education use Nandimobile's m-services (see Exhibit 1).

	Business Name	Type of Business / Industry	Product Being Used by Business
1.	Forever Claire (FC) Group of Companies	Beauty care, cosmetics	Gripeline Infoline
2.	ACCA Global, Ghana Office	Professional education	Infoline
3.	Pentecost Church Head Office	Religious	Infoline
4.	Vaniado	Homecare/sanitary	Infoline
5.	Preparation for Life (PFL)	Education	Infoline
6.	Starbow	Aviation	Infoline
7.	Multimedia Group (MyJoyOnline)	Media and Communication	Infoline
8.	International Central Gospel Church (East Legon Branch)	Religious	Infoline
9.	China Europe International Business School (CEIBS)	Education	Infoline
10.	Toyota Ghana Limited	Automobile	Infoline

Exhibit 1 Sample Institutions using NandiMobile's Products

NandiMobile's m-services, especially Gripeline, has received several local and international awards. For instance, during the Launch Conference in February 2011, panellists adjudged Gripeline as the best m-service, for its ability to connect businesses with their customers. Anne reckons that

> 'NandiMobile was given the award because of Gripeline's international replicability. Customer service is practiced everywhere, and so a solution like that would be useful anywhere'.

The company's growing worldwide reputation has culminated in several speaking engagements (allAfrica, 2012), and interviews. For instance, recently Anne received an invitation to join a handful of African women entrepreneurs to interact with Fortune's Most Powerful Women Leaders to share their time, talent and expertise in business and leadership (US Embassy, 2013; enewsgh.com, 2013). Nandimobile's activities over the three years has seen the Mobile Business Organisation (MBO) breaking even and not needing any more funding from MEST (see Exhibit 2 for the company's financial profile). Michael shares that

> 'Nandimobile has been running on its own funds for more than a year now and has not received any round of funding [from MEST]'.

	2010	2011	2012	May 2013
Net Profit After Tax (both Infoline and Gripeline) in Ghana Cedis	-	-	41,866	Not given to author
Number of Infoline Subscribers	4	24	66	49[1]
Number of Gripeline Subscribers	2	-	-	1
Number of Employees	3	5	7	8

Exhibit 2 NandiMobile's Financial Profile

Edward reveals that,

> 'Nandimobile broke even in the middle of last year (2012), and started making profits (thereon)'. 'In general, the ICT industry in Ghana is profitable depending on whether you focus on a need that can be satisfied with your product or service'.

Nandimobile's profile suggests the existence of some information system (IS) resources including IS technical skills and IS development. The MBO has resources like the Technical Manager and Mobile Applications developer. The company is also engaged in the creation of mobile services (m-services) like Infoline and Gripeline. Therefore, there is the presence of IS technical skills and IS development respectively.

Nandimobile M-Business Services

Nandimobile has three main m-services. These are *Gripeline, Infoline,* and the *Business Directory*. Gripeline, Nandimobile's first product, is a web-based Customer Relationship Management (CRM) service, which runs on SMS. Gripeline allows customers to have instant and continuous communication with companies who can also provide instant feedback. This m-service incorporates the advantages of SMS and Nandimobile's advanced technology to connect businesses and customers in the most personal and engaging way. With this service, businesses are able to provide a two-way communication channel for their consumers via mobile i.e. using an online interface, the organisation's representatives can respond to the questions that consumers ask via SMS. The same interface also allows companies to monitor and analyse the content of the messages received. Gripeline can be described as an m-service which is interactive. In other words, firms can send and receive messages to and from other mobile phone users instantly. Since Gripeline is Nandimobile's service, we could say that this mobile business organisation had an interactional m-business capability to create such an m-service.

Nandimobile's second m-service, *Infoline*, enables businesses to enhance their communication with their consumers. When a business subscribes to Infoline, they receive a short code through which they can send an automated preset feedback to mobile phone users who make enquiries about their products or services. Infoline opens up companies to be reached via mobile i.e. text messages. The service also aggregates and organises customer messages in a dashboard to provide a regular view of customer needs. Infoline offers some advantages including an affordable and efficient marketing platform which allows companies to do *Keyword Marketing*. This means that companies can include a mobile short code (e.g. 1945) in the advertisements they run on billboards, television, or radio. A keyword is a unique word assigned to a company [who subscribes to Infoline], which consumers can send to the mobile short code to receive an appropriate response. Selorm explained that traditionally, consumers are sometimes unable to catch advertisers' phone numbers from advertisements be it radio, television or billboards. To provide a solution to this challenge, companies can rather subscribe to Infoline to receive a unique *keyword* which would be communicated in the advertisement. In other words, instead of asking consumers to call a ten-digit phone number which they are unable to record, they could rather text a four-letter keyword to a three- or four-figure mobile short code, in order to receive information. In so doing, the advertisers receive information about people who have interest in their product, and perhaps, place follow-up calls. Edward advises that, such a system

> *'...is very useful because, when the company is running a promotion, it can send notifications directly to people who have previously shown interest in their product/ service'.*

Moreover, Infoline allows the creation of multiple keywords for companies that advertise through different channels e.g. print media, and electronic media. Using multiple keywords allows such companies to track the performance of each of the different media through which the advertisements go. Infoline also allows companies to send SMS messages in bulk to many individuals at the same time and at competitive rates. Such messages could either be scheduled or sent immediately. The product also comes with a 'performance checker' known as 'Analytics'. On the product dashboard, a company can tell how many messages it has sent out over a period, how many responses it received per campaign, billing information, and the performance of company keywords. Information in the Analytics could be used to generate graphs, which companies can use to easily spot trends and areas for improvement. All these features are accessible over the Internet. According to Belinda,

> *'A company needs just a computer with Internet access. Others prefer to use smart phones'.*

Nandimobile assigns subscribing companies with a username and password to log onto Infoline's dashboard and features via the Internet. Infoline can be described as an m-service which is informational. Thus, businesses that subscribe to Infoline are able to send messages to their customers e.g. informing them about a promotion. They do not receive feedback from the recipients. Since Infoline is Nandimobile's service, we could say that this mobile business organisation had an informational m-business capability to create such an m-service.

Nandimobile has a third m-service called the Business Directory. This m-service enables mobile users to search through a list of businesses via SMS using their mobile phones. The directory's system returns results containing the business name, contact details, business address and the services delivered by the business the consumer searched. If the directory contains more than one entry with the name searched, up to five results are delivered for the user's convenience at no extra cost. The service offers an avenue for Ghanaian companies to list and make its information available to over fifteen million mobile phone users in Ghana. With over 90,000 listings, the business directory aims to be the first option for mobile users seeking information about businesses in Ghana. The service runs across all networks in Ghana and costs ten Ghana pesewas (10p) per search.

To access the service, a user sends FIND [Name of Company] to short code 1945. The results are delivered to the users' handset. Unlisted businesses can enter their information into the directory by registering on the NandiMobile website. Someone from NandiMobile audits and adds the information to the business directory. If any company's information is not found, there is an option to go online and add that company's information. Since information from the business directory is only accessible upon a query, we can say that this service is interactional; hence, Nandimobile used their interactional m-business capability to create it.

Infoline and Gripeline were novel at the time of inception and launch. However, several content providers have similar offerings. Nevertheless, what makes Nandimobile's offer unique is the ability to combine their competitors' m-services. For instance, some value added service providers separately; i) offer bulk SMS services to their clients e.g. Rancard Solutions, ii) provide business directory services e.g. Business Ghana, and iii) provide mobile short codes for consumers to interact with businesses e.g. SMS Ghana. However, Edward touts,

> 'NandiMobile is the only company that has identified these three things as essential to the consumer, and put all in one basket. So from one application, you can chat, you can search through 90,000 businesses for their contact information. Thus, depending on which part of our business model you look at, you will have one company doing that, but not doing all three.'

In summary, we have seen from the descriptions of the three m-services that Nandimobile has two main m-business capabilities i.e. informational, and interactional.

A Learning Experience

TiGo, the third largest mobile network operator in Ghana (see Table 5.1) approached NandiMobile in July 2010 to sign up for a pilot test of Gripeline. Specifically, TiGo wanted to use Gripeline for customer service and support of TiGo Cash – the mobile money arm of TiGo. According to the concept document Nandimobile drafted for TiGo, the project was for an SMS-based customer support application for use by the TiGo Cash customer support call centre agents. Traditionally, customers have to dial continuously in an attempt to establish a connection to a customer service agent of mobile network operators like TiGo. Sometimes, people wait a long while before receiving service. Gripeline was to be a solution to customers' frustration, by providing an alternative channel for customer support. According to Edward,

> 'TiGo wanted it not as a replacement for their voice-based call centre, but as an alternative. They wanted to start with TiGo Cash, and if it goes well, roll it out to all services'.

Even though the initial concept was what attracted TiGo, the design did not fully meet their needs. The initial design simply enabled back-and-forth real-time communication between a company and its customers via short messaging service (SMS). TiGo, wanted something more than that. The seeming deficiency of the original Gripeline to meet TiGo's need was because of inexperience with customer call centres. To make up for it, TiGo invited Nandimobile's team to study the processes of their call centre in Accra. Edward concedes that,

> 'They took us to their outsourced customer service unit where we sat down with the customer service agents, and we understood what went on there. It confirmed my assumptions and we had to throw away some'

The TiGo exposure resulted in an expansion of Gripeline's features. For instance, Nandimobile added the following features

- Trouble Ticket System: this feature tracks the detection, reporting and resolution of customer complaints, by allocating numbered tickets.
- Automated Ticket Distribution System: this feature automatically distributes queued tickets to customer service agents logged in at the time the ticket is generated. The distribution is done according to company choice i.e. whether

a ticket should be assigned equitably or to the next free agent, no matter how many complaints he/she has dealt with.
- Escalation Manager: this feature enables an agent to transfer a complaint to either a superior or a colleague who can deal with it better.
- Reports & Analytics Manager: this feature generates metrics for measuring the performance of customer service agents.
- Knowledge-based Manager: this feature manages information resources that customer service agents can use to provide responses to customers.

TiGo made two more requests. The first was for an analytics feature that enables the identification of the most prevalent word(s) in customer complaint messages. This is similar to identifying 'trending' words in the online micro-blogging platform, Twitter. Second, TiGo wanted a service which did not require the customer to pay – to access customer support via SMS. *'They wanted a toll-free version of the application',* Edward remembers. However, Nandimobile advised against that because *'...it will encourage spamming'*, he added.

Unfortunately, all the tweaking, redevelopment and enhancement Nandimobile did to Gripeline came to naught. In other words, the project was not implemented because, TiGo Cash's General Manager, Mr. Khuen How Ng, who was spearheading the project at the time, was reassigned to another TiGo country office. Whilst Khuen's successor did not seem enthused about the project his predecessor started, there was not much documentation either – apart from the initial and revised concept documents. At best, Khuen's successor asked that the entire process be restarted.

Nandimobile depended on the relationship previously built with TiGo Cash's Technical Specialist, and Mr. Khuen's aide, Ebo Jackson to make some progress in getting the project back on track. That effort did not go far either as Ebo left TiGo to join a rival mobile network operator, Vodafone. Further, as per TiGo company regulations, it was unethical and unacceptable for anyone to contact past (TiGo) employees about business done with them when they worked there. The gravest source of worry was the lack of documentation about the stages and actions taken about the project when Mr. Ng was in charge. Thus, the project had to be forgone.

> *'That was our first pilot, so we learnt a lot from it. That is how come we know about escalation –it was a way to know and understand the industry',* Edward shares in contentment.

In summary, we could see that in addition to Nandimobile's existing IS resources – IS technical skills and IS development, the MBO gained another resource i.e. managing external resources (Wade & Hulland, 2004). This resource lies in the MBO's relationship with key personnel at TiGo Cash during the initial phases of the proposed project. Further, even though the TiGo project did not come off, we could observe that learning took place. It is worth noticing learning, because it is a key aspect of the dynamic capability development process in any organisation. For instance, the learning experience informed the redesign of Gripeline, which in itself is an aspect of the capability development process – recombination.

Near Success

Exit TiGo, enter the Centre for Gender Studies and Advocacy (CEGENSA). Whilst TiGo was Nandimobile's first non-paying customer, CEGENSA, a gender rights advocacy centre based at the University of Ghana – became the first paying customer. The Centre was executing a project funded by the ARK Foundation; and wanted a platform over which students could report incidents of sexual abuse. One of the CEGENSA staff members had recommended NandiMobile's service. The Centre's readiness sped up the process of creating the first Infoline account. However, after setting up the product and agreeing on terms of use, the project did not take off. Edward recalls that,

> 'For some reason they never launched, but they paid for the software (Infoline). They said it got some diplomatic barriers; whoever had to approve were male lecturers and they thought it was...'

This event in Nandimobile's lifecycle is an example of how activities within the environment or ecosystem can affect the success or otherwise of an MBO's activities. In addition, this event and the TiGo experience suggest the importance of readiness on the part of all necessary stakeholders for the success of MBOs' activities.

Reconfiguring Existing Capabilities

Some months after the CEGENSA experience in 2011, Nandimobile prospected for the next client. Edward, doubling as Sales Manager at the time, contacted the Association of Certified Chartered Accountants (ACCA, Ghana). He explained to them what Infoline could help them do. Nandimobile's ability to spot a specific need that their application could satisfy was a basis for ACCA signing on; ACCA needed to send notifications to their members and examination candidates via their mobile phones. Over the period when ACCA used Infoline, it requested for some extra features. They wanted to be able to send precomposed messages with varying placeholders to different people at the same time.

> 'This is known in industry parlance as tagging,' Edward educates.

Thus, for instance, if 50 new candidates register with ACCA, messages would be sent to all 50. These messages even though they had the same structure, the student name, and account number, and examination date would vary. Similarly, a doctor would also need tagging to send different appointment times to different patients. The tagging feature makes it possible for the Infoline application to select the variable part of a message from a Microsoft Excel sheet created by the sending institution, like ACCA. Since, this feature was not originally in Infoline, the application had to be modified to satisfy ACCA. Edward acknowledges it was important to satisfy their need and win their business because ACCA sent many messages, and thus generated income for Nandimobile. Within ACCA's request, Nandimobile also saw an opportunity of making recipients feel special, to increase personalisation, and go beyond making just the name distinct, depending on the client's preferences. '*Since we implemented tagging in June 2012, it has been very helpful, especially for ACCA*'. For Nandimobile, ACCA's satisfaction ensured continuous use, and business. Edward appreciates that

> 'They (ACCA) are (still) our customers and they use our software very well'.

Interestingly, cursory scans and reviews of companies that offer Infoline-like applications do not have tagging. For instance, SMS Ghana does not have tagging in their bulk SMS service, Edward assures. The ACCA experience suggests the need for MBOs to align m-services to client needs to ensure client satisfaction.

Finding New Resources and Retiring Capabilities

After securing the ACCA deal, the three co-founders saw the need to expand Nandimobile's sales activities. As Edward intimates, Nandimobile recruited three sales officers. The purpose of bringing on the sales officers was to build a sales team for the mobile service. After three months, two were confirmed, whilst one was fired for lack of performance. In October 2012, management promoted the two hired sales officers to Sales Manager positions. They were to recruit one sales officer each to form two sales teams. Both sales teams were to report to Edward, the Business Development Manager. In April 2013, one of the sales managers resigned. He left Nandimobile for another company apparently a competitor.

The decision to build a sales team is congruent with the tenets of the founding stage within the capability development lifecycle. At the stage, a firm identifies a need to acquire a resource. In addition, asking the confirmed and promoted sales managers to recruit two more sales officers suggests a revisit to the founding stage.

Developing New Resources

The newly formed sales team adopted a proactive approach in prospecting for new clients, with a focus on corporate institutions. The strategy was to target businesses because it was a bit difficult to get individual customers to use the current applications apart from the business directory. Anne explains that

> '...the companies use the web application, they are our main target. We target the companies to target their customers; we don't target the customers directly, at least as at now'.

To this end, the sales team identifies possible companies that may have need for Nandimobile's m-services. The normal targets are those institutions with large customer bases like schools and churches who have students and congregations respectively. The team scans through Nandimobile's business directory for the contact information of potential businesses, and makes initial contact via a phone call. A team member explains the purpose of the m-service to the business, and arrange for a possible product demonstration. Selorm, the (remaining) Sales manager intimates that

> 'It is during the demonstration that they see how it works and get the full understanding of what it does'.

Sometimes, the demonstrations do not lead to immediate acceptance of and subscription to the m-service. Nevertheless, apart from the phone contact, and demonstration, other businesses contact Nandimobile based on referrals from existing clients or as follow-ups to previous contacts. When a client finally expresses interest in using the m-service, the sales team assesses their particular need and creates a one-month trial account for that business (see Exhibit 3 for an illustration of the process of subscribing to Nandimobile's m-service). After the trial, the business can choose to subscribe to one of the full packages (see Exhibit 3).

A field trip with a three-member sales team (made up of a driver, Selorm, and Belinda) revealed that the team constantly looks out for possible clients by taking notice of billboards, signposts and buildings for contact information. Sometimes a team member places a reconnaissance call while on the journey. Other times, the contact information is saved for later pursuit.

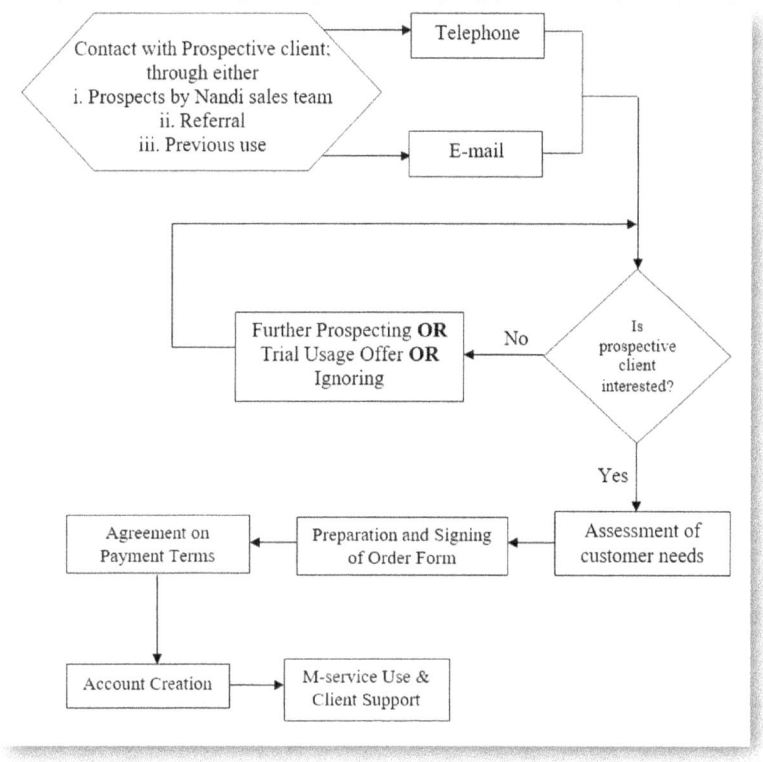

Exhibit 3 The Process of Subscribing to a NandiMobile Service

Nandimobile's proactive nature led to reaching a deal with FC Beauty Klinik, hereinafter referred to as FC. It was not very easy and smooth clinching that deal. It began with a phone call to the customer service desk at FC, to give a vivid description of the products and how they could be used in FC's operations. Selorm recalls,

> 'the customer service representative was not very enthused, but promised to forward the information to the CEO.'

FC's CEO called back after about thirty minute asking for a demonstration of the m-services' features and functionalities. The sales team quickly drove over to meet Grace, the CEO for a product demonstration. Even though she seemed fascinated with the products, she was quite diffident about the specific benefits the products held for her business, because she was already interacting with her clients using fixed telephone lines. How then could the sales team make the product look more beneficial to FC, Selorm reminisces asking himself and his team. It took a careful study of FC's operations to prepare a detailed training programme and manual specific for their needs. The study seems perpetual because FC keeps introducing new products and new units. The negotiations and constant support Nandimobile provided, yielded in FC's subscription to both Infoline and Gripeline. Whilst the cosmetic and beauty firm uses Infoline to send marketing messages via SMS to clients' mobile phones, it uses Gripeline to chat with customers towards solving their complaints. Two issues cropped up especially from the use of Gripeline. Over time, it seemed that Gripeline lost its relevance to FC. Selorm concedes that...

> 'If you report a skin issue for instance, the first thing they have to tell you is to come to the clinic. Hence, they did not need a dedicated person/employee to man Gripeline as the system's concept required.'

Capability Retirement
This observation of Gripeline's seeming irrelevance to FC caused Nandimobile to focus on just Infoline for the beauty company. Selorm adds that, *'Gripeline was not relevant (to FC), so we changed, and focused on Infoline'*. Currently, Nandimobile still provides support for Infoline at FC to encourage the use of the application. For instance, Nandimobile advised the CEO to add their keyword (i.e. FCBK) and shortcode (i.e. 1945) to all their advertisement channels. FC adhered. They advertise their keyword and short code in a coloured full-page advertisement they place in a weekend newspaper, the Mirror, regularly (see Exhibit 4).

CHOICES, CHANCES AND CHANGES - DOING BUSINESS IN GHANA

Source: The Mirror newspaper | 18 May, 2013 pg 9

Exhibit 4 Sample FC Advert with Keyword and Short Code

Following the newspaper advert by texting *Grace* and a question to 1945 or by sending *FCBK* to the same short code, one receives a message with contact numbers to call to book a free consultation (see Exhibit 5).

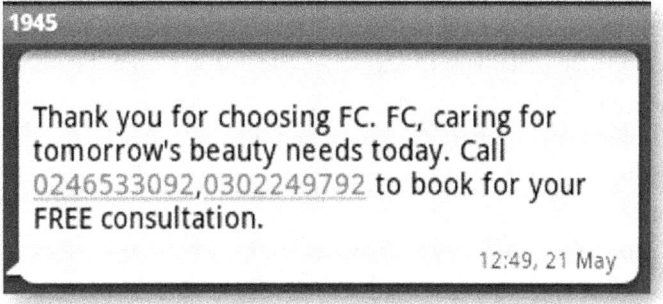

Exhibit 5 Sample Response from Texting FC's Keyword to 1945

Nandimobile's discontinuance of Gripeline at FC suggests retirement, which is one of the six possible paths which a firm's capability can take. It is retirement because, the capability seems to be discarded.

Capability Renewal

Apart from Nandimobile's proactive approach to increase its client base, sometimes other organisations contact the MBO with contracts. One such contract came from the British Council (BC) in October, 2012. Nandimobile received an e-mail from BC's Project Delivery Support office requesting a proposal to develop and implement an automated SMS information querying system for an education fair. The fair dubbed 'The *Education UK* Exhibition in Ghana' is a gathering of over thirty UK universities and colleges where mostly Ghanaian students and young professionals come to seek study and training opportunities.

BC expected Nandimobile or any of the other two companies invited to present a proposal to design, develop and implement an m-service which has

- a corporate bulk SMS system,
- a live SMS customer information querying system via short code to which participants can text across all networks,
- a database that British Council could monitor at any time.

Nandimobile's Infoline formed a solid foundation to deliver the application that British Council (BC) requested. However, the specific requirements called for some new features. Edward recalls that,

> *'British Council was very particular about our ability to provide them with hourly updates on the number of people who had actually turned up for the exhibition'.*

Apparently, Nandimobile won the contract because the other bidders were unable to add the functionality to provide hourly updates. This feature called for the development of a database that BC could monitor at any time. With dedication from Nandimobile staff, this was added easily. In January, 2013, the Nandimobile demonstrated the m-service to BC, and received selection notification to implement the service in February, 2013. The successful execution of the m-service for BC made it possible to design and sell a similar product to PFL, another institution that organises educational programs and university recruitment to Australian and some UK-based universities and colleges.

From the m-service provided to the British Council, we see that Nandimobile did not have that specific service already available. However, the MBO's existing m-service i.e. Infoline went through a new development stage to modify it to suit a new situation i.e. British Council's need. This suggests renewal of the ability to create Infoline – which was renewed to meet a new need.

Resource Reconfiguration

At certain times within the company, there is reduced need for technical activity. This means that there is not much need for programming and development activities. For instance, between April and June 2013 there was no product development activity. Whilst the technical team was doing routine maintenance for existing services, the rest of the staff was concentrating on sales. Michael who is part of the technical team and in charge of designing user experience shared that,

> '...product development is redundant now. I was leading the product development side of things, which means concepts, definition of product goals, and product synergy. Now I think we've achieved that. I am not really active in the company now, I am only working at the director level. When there is a need for product development, I come down from the director position to help out'.

This is not a single occurrence. We recall that in the early days of the company, Edward served as both Business Development Manager and Sales Manager until the firm formed a dedicated sales team. Similarly, Michael moves between roles as a director and a member of the product development team. This suggests resource reconfiguration when circumstances require it.

Challenges

Nandimobile's business journey has not been all-smooth. Anne, mentions that in the beginning, the major challenge was to get people to understand the concept and to accept the software as it was. She explains that using Nandimobile's m-services involve people changing the way they do things. For instance, a firm agreeing to, and subscribing to use Infoline means that they have to give up previous means of contacting their clients, e.g. voice calls via fixed or mobile phones, and rather use text messaging.

> 'So in the beginning it was more of getting people to understand the value of the software and accepting it as it is', she adds.

The MBO faced another challenge in 'aligning' the firm's m-services to the specific needs of prospective customers. This is evident from the FC scenario that even though the concept of the m-service is novel and perceived useful, its final acceptance rests on the client. To go around this challenge, Selorm, shares that Nandimobile trains the customers to ensure proper orientation about the m-service's usefulness.

> 'This is mainly to help them accommodate and accept the new way of undertaking their business activities', he adds.

Whilst this challenge may be specific for Infoline, there were some challenges for Gripeline. Selorm, concedes that the application is very good in concept and on paper, but has some implementation challenges.

Edward succinctly agrees that first, Gripeline is more customer service focused. Most companies have a bigger budget for marketing, so they would rather invest in attracting new customers instead of retaining those they already have. He observes that,

> 'Ghanaians would not leave anyway. Therefore, it is easier to convince someone to invest in a marketing tool like Infoline, than a customer service product like Gripeline'.

Second, businesses that subscribe to Gripeline need to employ someone to respond to and manage the conversations that originate from customers' phones. This is unlike Infoline where the business knows when to send and expect information to and from clients respectively. Therefore, if the business does not have someone who can do this, they have to employ someone.

> 'So first of all they don't want to invest, and now after investing in the software, they have to invest in another person?'

We see evidence of this challenge in FC Beauty Klinik discontinuing the use of Gripeline. Selorm admits that Nandimobile...

> '...barely sells Gripeline now. It has even lost some relevance for FC who bought it early on, so we are now focusing on Infoline'.

In addition, even though Nandimobile's products could be useful in government institutions, Edward describes the perceived difficulty in getting a government institution to use an m-service. He cites Nandimobile's age as a possible hindrance in getting their service accepted. Therefore, with the limited resources available, they would rather concentrate on winning contracts to provide more and more services for non-governmental institutions instead of governmental ones. This would be the focus until a time when the company can afford to pursue some government contracts.

> 'It would pay to get our m-service there, but we don't have the manpower to focus on them yet', he comments.

The above challenging scenarios suggest some difficulty in getting businesses to use Gripeline because of the need for some investments into human resources and equipment, without which Gripeline cannot work. This suggests the need for readiness of the business to adopt an m-service. Thus, even though Nandimobile is ready, the unready state of a business hampers the uptake of the m-service. In addition, Nandimobile's decision to focus on private businesses, and postpone prospecting for government contracts is suggestive of possibly low strategic political management, i.e. the strategic actions which a firm plans for and enacts for the purpose of achieving maximum economic returns from its political environment (Oliver & Holzinger, 2008).

Current and Future Projects

During the first two years, Nandimobile has focused on improving the first two m-services i.e. doing more of the marketing messages and enquiries (where consumers and businesses can chat). In 2013, the focus was more on the business directory. Edward admits how there has not been much attention on the business directory until March 2013. The company promises new entries into the directory. There would be an app version of the business directory too.

One main reason for developing the app version of their m-services is that the firm is looking into the future. Michael discloses,

> 'We are just looking into the future; we can't do SMS forever. Two or three years down the line, SMS might be dying or might be dead'.

Even though the apps are under development, the company does not intend to discard the SMS version any time soon. Rather, management hopes to remain relevant with the types of m-services delivered; whether SMS-based or app-based.

In looking into the future towards the development of app-based m-services, Nandimobile recruited a new developer, Joseph, to shore up the technical team specifically in the development of Nandimobile *Connect*. According to Michael, *'Joseph joined Nandimobile to do backend coding for the app'*. Joseph's introduction into Nandimobile's technical team suggests that the firm found itself at the founding stage of resource development. There was the need for app development skills. Thus, Joseph was recruited. Further, this new resource has already begun working, developing apps. This observation also suggests that the technical team and non-technical team were working together in *coordination*. Continuous development of m-services for Nandimobile amounts to learning until it generates a new *m-business capability* which becomes part of the firm. Management's decision and support for looking into the future to develop app-based m-services suggests strategic intent. This is a new direction management wants to move the company; and the resources to achieve this could be acquired – i.e. they are *gettable* e.g. app-development skill.

Joseph also hints that in addition to the app, Nandimobile is working on a mobile web version of the business directory to cater for Internet-ready non-smart phones. The MBO perceives that a majority of mobile phone users have this type of phones. These projects have the potential to diversify the firm's initial focus on businesses only. Anne indicates that *'we might now target the (individual) customers with the mobile apps we are rolling out'.*

In March 2013, Nandimobile displayed the beta version of the app during a national blogging conference called BlogCamp. During the conference, Nandimobile registered and directed people to download and test the NandiMobile app. Within six weeks, Nandimobile released a newer version of the app (yet to feature on Google Play Store). Whilst the beta version could only i) search for an already listed company ii) search for directions to listed companies' locations, and iii) allow mobile users to add a company to the directory,

> *'the new version is extended such that if customers search for and find a company, they could go further to initiate a chat, if that company subscribes to our Infoline',* Edward explains.

The main reason for this extension is the realisation that the use of Gripeline would be incrementally costly to mobile users. They may have to pay (i.e. 10p per message) for sending several messages before an issue is resolved. Therefore using the app is intended to reduce this cost because there is no short code. Interestingly, this new feature has drawn attention from the country's second largest mobile network operator, Vodafone. The network has a non-governmental organisation called Vodafone Foundation, which has requested Nandimobile to brand *Connect* for the foundation's public health education initiative called *Healthline*.

Within the decision to bring back Gripeline from retirement to merge with the app version of the business directory, we see another renewal of the capability which Nandimobile used to create Gripeline. The ability to execute the Vodafone request also suggests Nandimobile's ability to meet client needs; demonstrated in the British Council project. The feat also suggests strategic direction; management decided to follow up and execute the Vodafone request. This was enabled by use of current firm resources, which we could describe as *gettable*. Apart from medical information which needs to be loaded into the app, Nandimobile already had the needed resources available to make the necessary changes.

During the course of gathering data for this case study, the study observed that a financial institution, First Capital Plus, was using Nandimobile's mobile short code i.e. 1945. However, management declined to comment on the details of that m-service due to a non-disclosure agreement between the two firms. The *Speedbanking* service allows the bank's customers to top-up their accounts using a scratch card. The bank's customer buys a scratch card with the desired amount, scratches it, and sends the revealed number to a short code i.e. 1945 (see Exhibit 6).

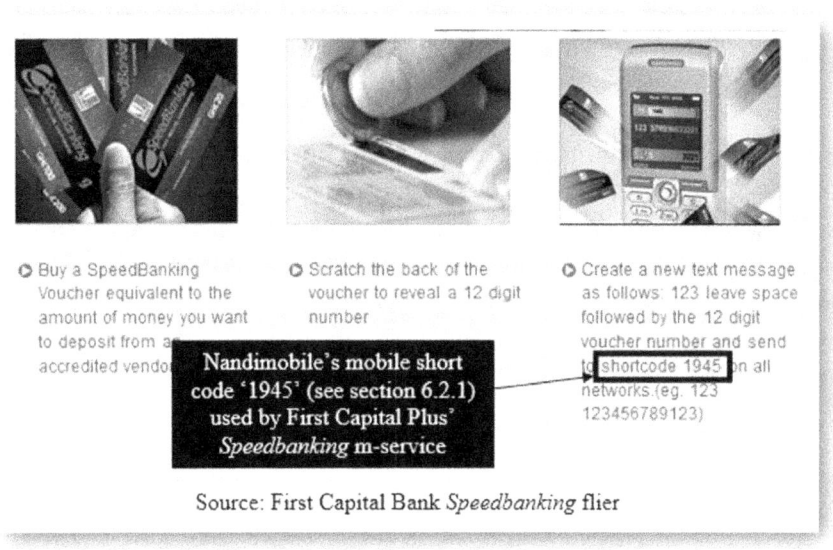

Exhibit 6 First Capital Plus' *Speedbanking* **m-Service**

The ability to create this m-service for First Capital Plus suggests a transactional capability; topping up a bank account via mobile could be regarded as a transaction. Even though Nandimobile would not comment on the m-service we could suggest that there was some modification of its existing m-service especially Infoline to create the Speedbanking service. This possibility also suggests a renewal of existing resources to suit a new situation. Furthermore, Edward's sustained belief in the viability of Gripeline informs a strategy aimed at making the m-service still useful. In short, it would be merged with Infoline. Businesses subscribing to Infoline need to request for it though. *'Therefore, if you buy Infoline, you are actually buying [Infoline] with or without Gripeline. We are still on the merger'* he educates. Michael agrees that the two m-services can and should be merged. He thinks that The merger will give a human face to the messages that businesses send to customers. In fact, the merger is extending to all Nandimobile's m-services. *'Everything is coming together'*; Michael shares. In the sense that in addition to the business directory app (i.e.Nandimobile Connect) providing the user with information about businesses, the app can also enable the user to send instant messages to those businesses who are using Infoline. A company's position in search results would however be determined by their Infoline subscription status such that

> *'when you do a generic search for, say, food joints, the results will display those who are Infoline subscribers first. It will be an ecosystem controlled by us. Thus even though you download the app for business information, we give you more',* Michael assures.

Nandimobile management's intention to merge their m-services suggests strategic direction. The firm realises some opportunity of which it can take advantage. To this end, it is combining existing m-services. This combination suggests a reconfiguration of resources. Currently, Nandimobile is displaying the capability to develop and experiment with app development which is a new form of mobile technology. Overall, we see different resources, existing and newly acquired, coming together to help achieve firm goals.

Questions

1. What resources do Ghanaian mobile services providers use to develop m-business capabilities to create mobile services?
2. How do Ghanaian mobile services providers develop and deploy resources to create capabilities in order to create m-services?
3. What is the impact of m-business capabilities on Ghanaian mobile service providers?

His Presence Hotel Limited: Appreciating People And Acting Responsibly

Kwamena Minta Nyarku and Dasmon Alex Akpabli

> This case study documents the history, the corporate social responsibility initiatives and human resource issues of a hotel operating in an African country, Ghana.

History and Company Profile

'What a wow', exclaimed one of the employees, as he saw his boss alight from his car that had just been parked in front of the hotel. Whenever His Presence Hotel Limited founder, Alex Akpabli arrived at the hotel premises, everyone met him with a smile as he exchanged pleasantries with all his management staff and employees. Alex is a results-oriented, hardworking and friendly individual, and is well known for his motivation, energy, enthusiasm, quest for success and drive throughout many different industries in Ghana. In May 2006, and about ten years ago, he founded His Presence Hotel Limited, a subsidiary of the Daasco Group of Companies - ranging from visual presentation systems, hotels, broadcast and telecommunication, automobile hiring, forex bureaus, and health improvement equipment. The hotel has a workforce of 25 employees in Ghana. It was incorporated on May 16, 2006 and certified to commence business on June 17, 2006. Customers love the hotel's service quality delivery and their cheerful energetic employees who love the atmosphere in which they work.

'We enjoy working here and we work hard to satisfy the needs of our customers', notes Linda Narh, one of the duty managers. Alex decided to step down as chief executive when he turned 60 years old. He created a successful organization and when he transferred power to Kwamena Minta Nyarku, the company was ready. 'It was an exceedingly orderly transition', said Alex.

As embedded in his corporate strategy, Alex was already preparing the company for change. When Kwamena took over as Chief Executive Officer, Alex noted that although Kwamena had previously maintained a low profile, he had been part of upper-level decision making for a *'long, long time and has been influential in shaping the direction of the Hotel'*. Anne, Alex's legal secretary moves into the position of chief operating officer at Daasco. Employees at other levels were – and continue to be groomed to take on more responsibilities. As one business expert and writer, Dr. Quaye, notes,

> 'These people have been in a leadership lab where they've had an opportunity to study and learn first-hand from Alex for many years. The company wouldn't be what it is today without them collectively.'

However, for companies with a wide array of services, a high percentage of the company's staff needs to understand the corporate sustainability objectives and consider these objectives throughout a large number of diverse research and development projects.

His Presence is a hotel that has built its business and corporate culture on the principles of total quality management (TQM). Customer focus, employee involvement, employee empowerment and continuous improvement are essential issues to His Presence employees and executives. Employees are included in business strategy planning, selected for their team skills, cross trained in a variety of areas, and are given the freedom to make decisions that will help customers and improve efficiency in any way they can. The company believes that the employees are the most valued assets of the company and therefore employs management by objectives (MBO) technique where managers and employees work together to set, record and monitor goals.

The company's recognition for corporate social responsibility (CSR) initiatives have been phenomenal over the years as its philanthropic activities have included unrestricted cash donations, donation of products, employee volunteerism, collection of customer donations, and charity events. Indeed, corporate philanthropy entails the ethical benefit of supporting others in need, gaining social status and a source of self-oriented, extrinsic value. Even when the economic conditions were adverse in 2008, the financial commitment of the Daasco Group of Companies towards social activities kept on increasing from GHS 20,000.00 in 1997-98 to GHS 30,000.00 in 1999-2000, and now GHS 1 million in 2015-16. It's not surprising that His Presence Hotel has been a winner of different CSR and performance awards.

Organizational Culture and HRM Practices

Inside His Presence Hotel, corporate culture plays a major role, as it promotes safety, customer satisfaction and consistency. Employees feel a sense of belonging as they work in teams and view their contributions to the success of the Hotel with unity and pride. Employees at all management levels are linked to the overall business strategy. The positive employee relationships enjoyed at His Presence Hotel are unusual in a hotel industry where antagonistic labour management relations are common. Organizational capabilities are key intangible assets.

As one business writer, Ramlall, puts it

'you can't see or touch them, yet they can make all the difference in the world when it comes to market value. Developing the capability or having the competency to respond effectively to changing customer needs ensures survival of an organization.

Companies' core competencies are able to produce a variety of business products in order to create ultimate value for themselves. His Presence Hotel always sees stakeholders as a source of competence.

The hotel, over the years, has developed a culture that treats employees the same way it treats its customers – by paying attention, being responsive and involving them in decisions at all levels. The company places high value on employees' enjoying their jobs, but places equal value on their performance. Employees are encouraged and trained to be flexible. And they are given lots of feedback about their performance. When they do well, they are duly and publicly recognized. Business practices as described above help position His Presence Hotel Limited as a company that can easily recruit and more importantly keep people. His Presence Hotel also instils environmental responsibility as a corporate value. Kailan, the assistant hotel manager noted that *'the way we have built our company by including everyone in the success of the company and not leaving our people behind is a great example of building a business the right way'.*

He further pointed out that

'the right way means truly turning employees into partners - shareholders with a stake in the outcome of the company'.

His Presence Hotel is committed to making a positive social contribution within the communities where it operates. It acknowledges its responsibility to engage with these communities by driving private public partnerships; being open and transparent over social investment initiatives including the amount of money, the reason for the investment and the beneficiaries; identifying and prioritizing strategic long-term partnerships; and developing mechanisms to ensure effective measurement of the impact of its social investments. The hotel won the Best CSR Company for Education award at the 5th Ghana CSR Excellence Awards, which recognizes best practices in corporate social responsibility. The award comes on the heels of other awards conferred on it in recent times by Industry watchers and stakeholders.

Upon receiving the award, Kwamena noted that

'sustainable CSR is an integral part of our company's culture – we execute with the aim of driving sustainable and measurable impact. For us, driving long-term sustainability across projects we support means being deeply involved, enabling our employees to volunteer and playing a key role in driving the change we want to see in our communities. This award is a validation of the effort we put in every day to transform education in Ghana'.

The Ghana CSR Excellence Awards in its fifth year is modelled after the European CSR Excellence Awards. It is presided over by a multi-stakeholder jury with reputable representatives from academia, business associations, regulatory agencies, civil society organisations and the media. The initiatives have helped to elucidate common misconceptions about CSR in Ghana, providing education and creating awareness about the global perspective of CSR within a local context. The Ghana CSR Excellence Awards have collaborations and endorsements from the Association of

Ghana Industries, Ghana Chamber of Commerce and Industries, Japan International Cooperation Agency, Plan International and the Ministry of Trade and Industry.

Industry's Recognition of Corporate Social Responsibility (CSR)

The hotel and tourism industry is amongst the world's fastest growing sectors and makes a 9% contribution to global gross domestic product (GDP) amounting to US $6.6 trillion (World Travel and Tourism Council, 2013 report). Also, according to a 2010 Deloitte survey, 34 percent of the surveyed travellers are now seeking for environmentally friendly hotels. Hoteliers have started to incorporate responsible business practices into their businesses and many hotels are committed to adopting the sustainability reporting practices in an effort to meet the demand for greater transparency.

While the hotel industry is neither responsible for severely polluting the environment nor accountable for consuming vast amounts of non-renewable resources, the industry has a significant effect upon the use of global resources, thus impacting on local communities through their occupation of space, use of infrastructure, and relationships with local businesses, communities and government. Indeed, international tourism associations are becoming increasingly active in responsible and sustainable issues and are ensuring high labour standards, promoting environmental sustainability and supporting local communities. CSR initiatives in the tourism and hospitality sector are becoming more significant, in line with other business sectors.

The hospitality industry is vast and very diverse. Any time people travel, stay in a hotel, eat out, go to the movies and engage in similar activities, they are patronizing establishments in the hospitality industry. The management of such establishments is very challenging, as managers need to be flexible enough to anticipate and meet a wide variety of needs. The practice of CSR is subject to much debate and criticism. Proponents argue that there is a strong business case for CSR, in that corporations benefit in multiple ways by operating with a perspective broader and longer than their own immediate, short-term profits. Critics argue that CSR distracts from the fundamental economic role of businesses; others argue that it is nothing more than superficial window-dressing; still others argue that it is an attempt to pre-empt the role of governments as a watchdog over powerful multinational corporations. A GTZ survey of Ghanaian companies showed that their efforts in this regard were rarely strategically planned, and generally philanthropic in nature. Companies reported that the two main reasons for their CSR activities were an interest in improving the company's image and a desire to promote the socioeconomic development of the most important stakeholders.

However, the same story is unlikely to be told about the hotel industry in Ghana, and being a significant sector, it has a crucial role in contributing to sustainability. The industry claims to embrace CSR, but it seems unclear how the companies integrate CSR activities into their core business and how they demonstrate real impacts and positive changes. Over the years, it has become apparent that many hotels in Ghana lack understanding of the concept of CSR. Previously, organizations considered CSR issues to be unnecessary; however, some organizations are beginning to recognize the importance of disclosure of information on CSR activities. Although the definitions of CSR differ, the general consensus is that it defines the duties of a company towards societal stakeholders and the environment, and that it describes how managers should go about managing these duties (Halme and Laurila, 2009). In Ghana, given the diversity of the concept, its understanding varies from industry to industry, indicating the voluntary nature of CSR initiatives, even after the launch of the Ghana Business Code in 2006 which provides comprehensive documentation on CSR in Ghana.

In 2013, Ghana's Ministry of Tourism with support from UNDP, UNECA and UNWTO implemented a 15-Year National Tourism Development Plan (2013-2027) to assess how tourism can contribute to national and local economic development via employment creation, revenue generation, environmental conservation and national cohesion and overall economic growth. Two main issues raised in the plan are branding and CSR. So, should hotels in Ghana respond to this growing phenomenon and be concerned about CSR practices? What are the potential benefits and risks, and should hotels act responsibly? In a competitive hospitality industry which offers homogeneous products and services, individual hoteliers must be able to satisfy customers better than their counterparts. The hotel's attributes such as cleanliness, prices, location, security, personal service, physical attractiveness, opportunities for relaxation, standards of service, appealing image, and reputation are recognized as decisive by customers to assess the quality of the hotel. In the past, companies have been practicing CSR but most of the time it has been viewed as something to fill annual reports and corporate public relations statements. In fact, it has never been taken seriously enough to make it a part of corporate business strategy.

Corporate entities in recent times have come under pressure to build public trust in order to be competitive in the global business environment. His Presence Hotel

Limited has responded to the clarion call by investing more resources and money into CSR activities in order to meet the needs of stakeholders such as society, employees, customers, communities, governmental agencies, and industry watchers.

In Ghana, Prof Hinson, a Professor of Marketing at the University of Ghana Business School, noted that,

'each company responds in its own unique way to CSR issues and the extent of their response is influenced by factors such as the specific company's size, the particular industry, the firm's business culture, and stakeholder demands and how historically progressive the company is in engaging in CSR'.

The Hotel has so far invested over GHS 1 million in different CSR initiatives. In the company's experience, and as noted by Kwamena,

'the best practice is not to view sustainability as a special initiative led by a separate team, but to integrate sustainability goals directly into our business plans and objectives'.

Classification of social responsibility

Indeed, many companies' initial CSR efforts end up not being sustainable. This is because the companies base decisions on doing the right things environmentally without quantifying the economic benefits over the long run. There are no shortages of CSR opportunities that have an attractive business case as well as doing something environmentally or socially commendable. CSR values, policies and objectives help communicate to internal and external stakeholders what really matters to the organization in a way that is visible, transparent and measurable. A key aspect of CSR is dialogue with and responsibilities to stakeholders. The notion of stakeholders enables a personalisation of responsibilities and also delineates the specific groups or persons' businesses should consider in its CSR orientation.

1. **Responsibility towards itself -** It is the responsibility of each company to run business and to work towards growth, expansion and stability and thus earn profits. If the company is to achieve social and economic ends, organizational efficiency should be improved. The company should recognize that profitability is essential to its future success, and should be addressed equally.

2. ***Responsibility towards Employees*** - Employees are the most important part of an organization, and responsibilities towards employees include - timely payment; hygienic working environment; good and impartial behaviour; health care; safe layout and workplace; recreational activities; great work environment; recognition of respect and dignity; embrace diversity; encourage them to take part in managerial decisions. Employees are constantly serving and meeting customers daily, and as such poor treatment of employees would likely affect the way they would serve customers.
3. ***Responsibility towards shareholders*** - It is the responsibility of the company to safeguard the shareholders' investment and make efforts to provide a reasonable return on their investment.
4. ***Responsibility towards state*** - Out of the profit available, the state is entitled to a certain share as per the income tax laws. Utmost transparency has to be exerted regarding the profit and loss account and the balance sheet.
5. ***Responsibility towards consumers*** - The company should maintain high quality standards at reasonable prices. It should not resort to malpractices such as hoarding and black-marketing.
6. ***Responsibility towards environment*** - It is the responsibility of the organization to contribute to the protection of the environment. It should produce eco-friendly products, manage waste properly, and contribute positively to both communities and the environment. Understanding environmental issues and sharing information with partners.

His Presence Hotel's CSR Strategy

Since 2006, His Presence Hotel has directly contributed to non-profit organisations' developmental projects. These include community service initiatives, employee community service projects, donated products to brilliant but needy tertiary students, constructed borehole projects, offered HIV/AIDS assistance program support to inmates at Ghana Prisons, adopted 4 orphanages in Ghana for educational sponsorship; embarked on tree planting exercises, and trained staff on health and safety issues. In March 2016, the company sponsored 3 sporting activities in 10 different communities, built 3 classroom blocks, refurbished lecture halls and auditorium at the Kwame Nkrumah University of Science and Technology (KNUST), funded the publication of books for Ghana Public Health, and sponsored the training of journalists on economic and financial reporting. It further made donations to the University for Development

Studies (UDS), and the University of Energy and Natural Resources, and has introduced many scholarship programmes for higher education.

In addition, the hotel donated uniforms, scholastic material (books, notepads, pens, etc.), textbooks, furniture (desks, chairs, etc.), mid-day meals, teacher incentives; government fees re-imbursements, and teaching and learning aids to its adopted schools. The company has planted 8,000 trees and 3,000 trees in the Central and Volta regions respectively. Societies have been formed for rural development and for providing healthcare to the rural areas. These societies have made great efforts for health, education and women empowerment in rural areas.

His Presence Hotel believes its strong commitment to CSR benefits both the company and its stakeholders. Some of the benefits include attracting and retaining partners (e.g. comprehensive benefits package that motivates workers and safe and healthy workplaces), customer loyalty (customers associate His Presence Hotel with good corporate citizenship and often recommends their services to friends and family), reducing operation cost, and creating a sustainable supply chain for its own future growth.

We have made significant investments in our supply chains, with the long term in mind. Our focus has been to ensure that our suppliers of today will have the capacity to supply His Presence Hotel business tomorrow.

The Hotel has a strong sense of shared accountability for CSR with shareholders, and the board of directors hold management accountable to operate and comply with the company principles (CSR, 2012). Kailan, again acknowledges that

> 'CSR to us simply means conducting business in ways that produce social, environmental and economic benefits not only for our company but for all stakeholders. Not only doing well for a person but also for the environmental issues, communities, and charity activities which focuses on service quality delivery, society, environment and employees'.

A Look Toward the Future

In 2010, the company announced that in future, it wasn't going to deal with companies that do not comply with its CSR standards and has amended its sustainable clause to read as 'His Presence Hotel shall be committed to be a good corporate citizen by actively assisting in the improvement of the quality of life of the people in the communities in which it operates with the objective of making them self-reliant. It hopes to initiate and support community initiatives in the field of community health and family welfare, water management, vocational training, and also encourage volunteering amongst its employees to work in the communities'.

This will be reviewed periodically in consonance with national and regional priorities, and would strive to incorporate them as an integral part of its business plan. In this sense, a change of paradigm is being evidenced, together with the uprising of a new line of thinking. And as noted by Kwamena,

> 'the commitment of employees and in particular decision-makers is essential to successful CSR', and further hinted that 'CSR needs proper and step by step implementation'.

Despite the consistent depreciation of the cedi in relation to other currencies and customer sophistication, the hotel sought for ways to encourage the public to patronise its facilities and services. Many loyalty programmes, credit and hiring policies have been developed to help many customers appreciate the services and brand. The Hotel looks forward to opening more branches across the country. 'They are doing what they do best, which is to shine in the hours of trouble', noted Francis Nutsugah, President of Daasco's automobile hiring firm. 'This to me is not a gamble but a strategic move.'

Still, Chief Financial Officer Mike Addo cautioned that the company 'would not be making any outrageous moves but is thinking both strategically and tactically.' Its commitment to local communities is to align resources and leverage technology to support young social entrepreneurs who are seeking to change their communities through innovative ideas and volunteerism. Kwamena asserted that

> 'hotels should be environmentally sensitive, have a deeper sense for the community, respect their culture and diversity, be open for dialogue and bring decentralized decisions. At the same time, they should be open and ready for innovations in order to keep their position in the ever challenging industry and to compete. This is the way they could enhance economic growth and increase the competitiveness of the industry'.

Different hotels in the world have accepted the challenge of sustainable development to be one of their priorities when doing business. The Government of Ghana (GoG) is developing a national policy on CSR to ensure that institutions promote the welfare of communities in which they operate. While the absence of such a policy has resulted in inconsistent CSR practices over the years, national public lectures are changing things for the better. So far as hotels continue to consume water, energy, food, paper, linen, consumables, stationery, cleaning materials and other resources, while generating air, water, soil and noise pollution impacting on local communities, CSR will continue to be debated, considered and adopted.

Questions

1. Examine His Presence Hotel's CSR strategies and identify their respective CSR classifications.
2. Identify, and using relevant examples, explain three values that the organizational culture of His Presence Hotel promotes.
3. Why would you want to work for His Presence Hotel Limited? Outline three reasons.
4. Do you think that His Presence Hotel's success is more as a result of socially responsible practices, human resource practices or the interaction between the two? Can human resource practices help a company be successful without being socially responsible?

Acknowledgments:

The authors' heartfelt acknowledgements go to Mr. Alex Akpabli, CEO and Chairman of Daasco Group of Companies; Management and Employees of Daasco Group of Companies and His Presence Hotel Limited; and Mrs. Lorraine Dei-Minta Nyarku, Human Resource Manager at La Palm Beach Resort Hotel, for their support and advice in developing and writing this case study.

References and Additional Readings

Abdolvand, M. & Charsetad, P. (2013). Corporate social responsibility and brand equity in industrial marketing, *International Journal of Academic Research in Business and Social Sciences*, 3(9). 273.

Abouzkeh, A. & Kamla, R. (2013). *A critical perspective on social accounting in banking*. PhD Thesis, University of Dundee.

Alexander, A., Francis, A., Kyire, L. A. & Mohammed, H. (2014). The effect of corporate social responsibility on brand building. *International Journal of Marketing Studies*, 6(3). 126.

Assaf, A. G., Josiassen, A. & Cvelbar, L. K (2012). Does triple line reporting improve hotel performance? *International Journal of Hospitality Management*, 31(2), 596-600.

Boonpattarakan, A. (2012). Model of Thai small and medium sized enterprises' organizational capabilities: review and verification. *Journal of Management Research*. 4 (3).

Chan, E. S. W. (2011). Implementing environmental management systems in small and medium-sized hotels: obstacles. *Journal of Hospitality & Tourism Research*. 35(1), 3–23.

Chan, E.S.W. & Wong, S.C.K. (2006). Motivations for ISO 14001 in the hotel industry, *Tourism Management*. 27(3), 481–492.

Chung, L. H. & Parker, L. D. (2010). Managing social and environmental action and accountability in the hospitality industry: A Singapore perspective. *Accounting Forum*. 34, 46-53.

Crane, A., Matten, D., & Spence, L. (2008). *Corporate Social Responsibility: Readings and Cases in Global Context*, London: Routledge

De Grosbois, D. (2012). Corporate social responsibility reporting by the global hotel industry: commitment, initiatives and performance. *International Journal of Hospitality Management* 313, 896–905.

Halme, M. & Laurila, J. (2009), 'Philanthropy, integration or innovation? Exploring the financial and societal outcomes of different types of corporate responsibility. *Journal of Business Ethics*, 84(3). 325-339.

Khairat, G. & Maher, A. (2012). Integrating sustainability into tour operator business: An innovative approach in sustainable tourism, *Tourismos: An International Multidisciplinary Journal of Touris*m, 7(1), 213-233.

Lee, E. M., Park, S.-Y. & Lee, H. J. (2013). Employee perception of csr activities: Its antecedents and consequences. *Journal of Business Research*, 66(10), 1716-1724.

Mandhachitara, R., & Poolthong, Y. (2011). A model of customer loyalty and corporate social responsibility. *Journal of Services Marketing*, 25(2). 122-133.

McCleary K.W., Weaver P.A., & Hutchinson J.C. (1993). Hotel selection factors as they relate to business travel situations. *Journal of Travel Research*, 32 (2), 42–48.

Millar, M. & Baloglu, S. (2011). Hotel guest's preferences for green guest room attributes', *Cornell Hospitality Quarterly*, 52(3), 302-311.

Ministry of Tourism, Ghana (2013) *National Tourism Development Plan (2013-2017)*, Accra, Ghana.

Molina-Azorin, J. F., Claver-Cortes, E., Pereira-Moliner, J., & Tari, J. J. (2009). Environmental practices and firm performance: an empirical analysis in the Spanish hotel, *Journal of cleaner production*. 17(5), 516-524.

Oberseder, M., Schlegelmilch, B. B., & Murphy, P. E. (2013). CSR practices and consumer perceptions. *Journal of Business Research*, 66(10), 1839-185.

Ofori, D. & Hinson, R. (2007). Corporate social responsibility perspectives of leading firms in Ghana. *Corporate Governance*, vol. 7(2). 178-19

Servaes, H. & Tamayo, A. (2013). The impact of corporate social responsibility on firm value: The role of customer awareness. *Management Science* 59(5), 1045–1061.

Sheldon, P. J., & Park, S. Y. (2011). An exploratory study of corporate social responsibility in the U.S. travel industry. *Journal of Travel Research*, 50(4), 392-407.

Suhartanto, K., (2000). Customer loyalty in the hotel industry: The role of customer satisfaction and image. *International Journal Contemporary Hospitability Management*, 12(6), 346-351.

Thompson, A., Peteraf, M. A., Gamble, J. E. & Strickland III, A. J. (2013). *Crafting and Executing Strategy: Concepts and Cases*. African Edition. New York: McGraw-Hill Irwin.

Vanacore, A. & Erto, P. (2002). A probabilistic approach to measure hotel service quality. *Total Quality Management*, 13(2), 165-174.

Wuest, B. E. S., Tas, R. F., & Emenheiser, D. A. (1996). What do mature travellers perceive as importanthotel/ motel customer service? *Hospitality Research Journal*, 20(2), 77–93.

CRM Implementation in a Ghanaian Real Estate Company

Gordon Kofi Sarfo-Adu and Gladys Nkrumah

The case offers a perspective into the relevance of customer relationship management (CRM) in a real estate company, how CRM is implemented, and how to circumvent implementation challenges.

Firm Profile

Building houses and flats for the people of Ghana is the main preoccupation of State Housing Company Limited (www.statehousing.com.gh). It has concerned itself with this arduous task since its inception in 1956 when it was called Gold Coast Housing Corporation and operated as the main housing development agency of the Government. In July 1995, the State Housing Corporation was converted to a limited liability company and now operates as a fully-fledged commercial enterprise. State Housing Company Limited (SHCL) has over the years achieved impressive landmarks in the real estate industry by providing affordable and quality housing estates. We have an enviable reputation for being the only real estate developer operating all over the country.

State Housing Company Limited is committed to the objective of being a nationwide profitable housing agency, which makes housing easily accessible to institutions and individual Ghanaians both home and abroad. It is Ghana's leading land developer and operates in a manner that contributes directly to the orderly and efficient development of the country's housing sector. This is effectively achieved through our reorganized operational structure which groups the regions into five zones; Head Office, Eastern, Western, Ashanti, and Northern.

VISION
Our vision is to provide high quality affordable homes in thriving communities where people have a sense of pride and place.

MISSION
To serve the housing needs of all income groups including those who do not have comparable housing options through conventional financial channels; developing over 1000 homes annually.

Background to the CRM Implementation

SHCL has previously kept a manual system of storing customer information. The closest use of technology was a spread sheet that is used to store some customer information while it continued to use hard files for most of the information. The sales team searched for leads and closed as many sales as possible. The team was also supposed to constantly stay in touch with customers and update them on the progress of their houses as well as provide them with feedback for any complaints they made.

In the year 2012, SHCL adopted a customer relationship management (CRM) system to facilitate the process of tracking and organizing customer contacts. The CRM system they opted for is web-based and supports both front- and back-office operations. It is intended to store relevant information readily for use by the Sales Team. The CRM software christened SIMS (Sales Information Management Systems) was sourced from a foreign based vendor, who was just an email away. When it was installed, the vendor sent a team to train the staff to be able to use it efficiently. The key managers who work with the system are the General Manager in charge of Marketing and Corporate Affairs, the Marketing Manager, and the Sales Manager. The company also has an Information Technology Department headed by a manager who largely provides only support services in the running of the CRM software.

Reasons behind the Adoption of CRM

Data on customers became huge and overwhelming, due to an ever increasing clientele base. It was becoming more and more difficult for Sales Agents to keep up with customer files, as well as follow leads. There was also the challenge of storage of these paper files. Basic customer information such as phone numbers and email addresses were not readily available. They had to be extracted from piles of files. Customer information contained on paper documents easily got misplaced while being shuffled between departments. Therefore, locating customer details for the purposes of follow ups was herculean and that greatly affected the ability of the Sales Team and other staff members to reach out to customers promptly. The Sales Manager who was working in the company before SIMS was deployed commented:

> 'Usually when clients need to be updated, especially with progress of their properties and then with payments, they do not receive updates as early as they would want to. This affects them in planning their finances and so they will be there and then may be a week for us to get to roofing level, Finance will send them a mail telling them that they would have to come and pay that same week'.

The company needed to track traffic to its website, and to know how many people, who they are, their geographical location, what they wanted when they visited the website, and how to translate that into leads and sales. Related to that was the need for a more comprehensive reporting of their sales activities and the need to interface developments at other departments with the Marketing and Sales Department. This would involve allowing designated managers, at a click of a button, to know what was going on in order to assess the company's performance at each point in time. The Marketing Manager noted:

> The software creates value for our operations, as it makes it easier for the company to manage its relationships with customers.

This is consistent with the claim by Saarijarvi *et al.* (2013) that firms largely embark on CRM, primarily to create value for their operations. Saarijarvi *et al.* (2013) argue that though firms tend to focus on their value, CRM implementation will be more successful, if firms place priority on customer value creation instead of the firm's operational value. The company settled on SIMS, which is basically a sales information management system used to manage customer relationships. This also confirms the findings of Payne and Frow (2005), who in explaining what CRM is, suggest that *'it is often used to describe technology-based customer solutions, such as sales force automation (SFA)'.*

Features of the Sales Information Management Systems (SIMS)

SIMS is tailored for the Real Estate industry, and stores consistent records of customers. The records in this data repository, helps to achieve personalized interaction with customers and are easily retrieved for reference by the Marketing and Sales team, as well as other key managers, who have accounts uniquely created for them. It is integrated into the website of the company, allowing the company to know who visited their website, for what purpose, how many times, from which location and whether the person is interested in any of their products and services.

The CRM software is hosted by the Head of the Marketing Department, who has a background in Digital Marketing. The system is supposed to contain every bit of information on customers and even leads. An account is created for each customer and the Sales Team is mandated to input every customer information into the system as well as notes on all calls and interactions held with a customer, from the first point of contact through to the purchase and handing over of the house to the customer. All documents including, land title, sub-lease, cost of the house, payments and receipts for each of the customers are scanned and uploaded. It also has another segment which allows for analysis of customer information. The Marketing Manager explains that with this analysis:

> *'You can take a look at how many homes are left to be sold, how many homes you have, how many homes are pending, so you can split it out into segments and it also gives you a reporting facility'.*

There are different access levels on the software. The Marketing Manager who is the administrator and other designated managers can see all the developments and all the reports captured in the system. But there is the Agent site, where the Sales Agent can only see his or her leads and then there is the administrator access level that allows for editing. Apart from making inputs, the designated officers of the company can also import and export information from the system. Significantly, this software is able to show a pictorial view of the layout of the various housing projects, as stated by the Marketing Manager:

'The SIMS system can put down every house within it, so we can see, which house is sold, you can see which house is available, which house is unsold and it can break it down into batches'

The company sees SIMS as a durable, easy to use system which is cost effective for big companies, because it is an expensive investment which may not be profitable for smaller firms. However, it is important to note that the CRM software is as rich with information as the Sales Team has uploaded.

Implementation Challenges

The implementation of the CRM system is to a very large extent nascent; none the less it is saddled with some challenges. They include the absence of a strategy to guide its implementation, as well as the challenge of entering the requisite information into the system.

The company, in rolling out the CRM software did not embark on any particular organizational restructuring and orientation, as Teo *et al.* (2006) and Payne and Frow (2005) recommend. There is also no CRM Strategy or Vision, though scholars have argued that these elements are necessary for its successful implementation. The company has just not found the need for a CRM strategy as they could not give any explanation for its absence. Literature reviewed suggests some common perspectives of CRM that should guide its implementation. They include the Strategic Perspective, Operational Perspective and Analytical Perspective. Scholars posit that for CRM implementation to be successful, the firm must adopt a holistic approach which would mean that all 3 perspectives must exist. The Strategic perspective would imply that the firm must have a CRM vision and strategy, and orient the staff of the company towards its implementation. The Analytical Perspective would mean that the CRM implementation must allow for data mining and be customer centric (Teo *et al.*, 2006), while the Operational Perspective has to do with the roll-out of 'customer-facing processes' (Payne and Frow, 2005). It could be said that the Real Estate Company has not considered the Strategic Perspective in particular in the deployment of SIMS.

Additionally, literature suggests that the CRM success rate is low. Frow *et al.* (2011) quote AMR Research (2007) that concludes that a third of every CRM deployment fails and less than half meet their goals fully and a major reason cited for this low success rate is the absence of a CRM strategy and orientation of staff (Teo *et al.*,

2006; Payne and Frow, 2005). On hindsight, the Sales Manager thinks they could have achieved a better result if there was a CRM strategy in place. She commented:

> 'If there was a strategy, I believe things will be different because everyone will know, ok... this is where we want to get to, this is our dream, this is what we want to achieve and so as much as possible how do we get there..., will all be part of the strategy'.

Suffice to state however that the Marketing Manager recognizes that the principle behind the implementation of SIMS is not just the software but its function as an enabler to assist the company to interact adequately with the customer.

Another challenge that the company contends with, is the prompt and proper entry of the required customer information. As a new system, compliance by the Sales Team to regularly enter customer information has been a major challenge. The Sales Team found the scanning and uploading of all customer documents and notes on interactions with them, as an extra time consuming responsibility. They consider the search for potential customers and closing of sales, which in itself is exacting, as their main duties and the entry of customer information into the CRM software as secondary. They therefore do not enter as much information and as regularly as required. The Sales Manager is certain that the Team is aware of the benefits of the CRM software and the need to populate it with information but she cannot exactly pinpoint why compliance has become so difficult to achieve:

> 'I don't know whether it has to do with the software....... or it has to do with us the human beings....We try to get them to use the software but....At a point in time the uploading goes on well and everyone is about SIMS, SIMS, SIMS...we'll all be updating our SIMS and then it gets to another point and it slows down again'.

The inconsistencies in uploading customer information, as well as the absence of a CRM Strategy have not enabled the company to derive optimum benefit of the software, although the management says significant gains have been made since it was deployed. What is required to be done is to maximize the benefit of the system and a number of actions and decisions taken by the management of the company, in the previous year, is targeted at navigating these challenges.

Efforts at Addressing the Challenges

Management of the company has been aware of the bottlenecks inhibiting the successful rollout of the CRM system. It has therefore taken a number of steps including training, mandatory entry of customer information, and recruiting people with the right skills set among others to try to overcome the setback.

The company in the previous year embarked on an aggressive training of staff members that handle the software, so that they can be conversant with it. The vendors did not send facilitators this time around because there are managers with the capacity to train the others. The General Manager, Marketing and Corporate Affairs, explained that a lot of effort went into the training programme to achieve a higher level of success. But the actual training for each staff, according to the Marketing Manager, takes just a couple of hours. He indicated that much of the efforts is in the mindset of the staff and particularly so with older employees.

> 'When it comes to older employees, you need to change their mindset to say this is a new process. Its web based. It is not that bad. It's a cool system and it's not that complex. It is more of a straight forward system, so if you use it right, you would get the result you want to get'

Every new employee that comes on board is trained. The Sales Manager also makes it a point to conscientize the Sales Team on the relevance of the system during their usual meetings.

Another solution to the identified challenges was a decision by management to make entry of customer information mandatory for all Sales Executives. The Sales Executives have specific number of customer contacts to make each day and every information that results from that interaction must compulsorily be entered into the CRM system. Also quality of data was rated and any data below 70 percent quality, (in terms of reliability and accuracy) was rejected and that went against the Sales Agent who made those entries. Furthermore, this requirement has been tied to the overall target of the personnel, which feeds into their performance appraisal. As a result of these managerial decisions, compliance has improved, according to the General Manager, Marketing and Corporate Affairs:

> 'Currently if you are a sales executive, you are supposed to input every discussion you had with anyone on the CRM. Actually they have been given targets. You must input, for now we are doing it three reports a day, so you are supposed to visit three people every day and put in reports...any sale you make, you upload'.

Despite the improvement in uploading customer information, the Sales Team is still unable to enter all the required information timely. The Sales Manager says there is backlog of customer information and documents yet to be uploaded. She admits though that there has been improvement but says the improvement is not as significant as management would have wished for.

Another measure the company will pursue in the near future, is to upgrade the CRM system. This will be done by developing other software applications for other departments such as the Estate, Development and Finance departments and interfacing them with SIMS. This is to ensure that any manager, who goes into the system can determine quickly the client type, the house type, design of the house, stage of development, documents of the customer, transactional activities with receipts, so that a holistic report can be generated easily. This will constitute an improvement because the Development and Estate Departments currently do not have their detailed information inputted into the system, although a significantly comprehensive report can be generated from it in its current state. The IT Manager also talked about plans to introduce a separate CRM system from a different vendor purposely for the Customer Service Department which will handle non-sales related customer service concerns. He said if it is compatible, it would also be interfaced with SIMS.

Benefits of the CRM system

Scholars have admitted to the difficulty in accurately measuring the benefits of CRM to a company. Vanini (2004) suggests that there is a major challenge in assessing the benefit of CRM and argues further that very few companies have tried to measure the cost and benefit of it. Scholars such as Ryals (2005) have made attempts at measuring CRM by using calculations of the Lifetime Value of customers in two longitudinal case studies, to prove that 'CRM activities deliver greater profits'. None the less, measuring the impact of CRM remains a challenge. The General Manager, Marketing and Corporate Affairs, was positive that their CRM has been beneficial but said no empirical assessment has been made, lamenting that:

'One time we were having a discussion on it and we were like if we could really quantify CRM, people will now realize the importance of customer service but you know we quantify finance, we quantify other things and it is easier but CRM is a little more difficult how much more the software, I think somebody can take it up as a project'.

The company believes that the following benefits have been derived, although they argue a lot more could have been achieved with a higher compliance rate. Increased sales from referrals could have been made as a result of better customer relationship management, enabled by the SIMS software. The company estimates that 80 to 90 percent of sales have been based on referrals from customers. Repeat purchase will normally not be a feature of a real estate company, as most people will even struggle to own one home in their life time and one will therefore be tempted to question the relevance of investing hugely in a CRM system. However, the customers of the company have become the 'part time sales force' to borrow from Gummesson (1996). The General Manager, noted significantly that it was better and cheaper to retain existing customers to secure their referrals than to go looking for a new customer. This claim is consistent with those made by scholars such as Grönroos (1994) as well as Sheth and Parvatiyar (1995):

'We know that those who have bought from us, it is easier and cheaper to keep them than trying to find another person to buy. So the Sales Executives in-house are chasing all the clients to make sure that they buy again. So, so long as you are in our system, for sales purposes, there will be a sales person covering you after you have finished purchasing and you have moved in or rented out your house. From time to time, they will call you; they will follow you at least once within a quarter. If they are doing that, what happens is, they know the people who can buy and so recommendations come. And so our sales is mainly on referrals.'

The management also says on the average, 40 percent of the company's sales is attributable to the CRM system, when in previous years, advertising and related marketing activities accounted for the lead sales. The CRM system has also brought about efficiency in the operations of the company. Data storage is better, more sales are closed by Sales Agents within a shorter time compared to the manual system. Fewer numbers of people is required for the same job set, and a comprehensive report can be easily generated and accessed from any point on the globe which was not possible in the past. The System also allows for personalized interaction with each customer, as customer information is readily accessible compared to the previous times that they used manual systems.

Closely related customer information is not lost with employee attrition, as the Sales Agents are mandated to key in every customer information, documents and notes on interactions into the system. As a result, any person who takes over the customer account is as good as the one that left. The backlog of data yet to be uploaded however poses a threat to this advantage.

The CRM system also brings about transparency, as activities of the various Sales Agents and other designated staff, are in the system for all to see. This avoids customer or lead duplication, as no two Sales Agents can be working on the same leads without the system detecting it, according to the Marketing Manager. Closely related is the fact that, the performance of the Sales Agents can be properly monitored to determine if they are meeting their targets and are responding adequately to customer needs and complaints, because their managers have access to that information on a daily basis.

Finally, the company is able to better manage the relationship with its customer, as a result of the earlier points discussed. The real estate company has several awards, both local and international to its credit and hopes to ride strongly on the back of good customer care and effective management of their relationship with the customers to chalk other successes. It is also hopeful that the CRM system implementation challenges will be resolved or reduced to the barest minimum over time. The company prides itself in good customer relations. Its head office, located on the Spintex Road, Accra, has a very welcoming ambiance and warm staff, who will constantly offer any visitor, water to drink. It has a youthful workforce even at the managerial level.

Questions

1. Identify the key management issues that confronted the firm and what steps were taken to address them?
2. State two measures that the firm can take to make CRM even more beneficial?

References

Frow, P., Payne, A., Wilkinson, I. F., & Young, L. (2011). Customer management and CRM: addressing the dark side. *Journal of Services Marketing*, 25(2), 79-89.

Grönroos, C. (1994). From marketing mix to relationship marketing: towards a paradigm shift in marketing. *Management decision*, 32(2), 4-20.

Gummesson, E. (1996). Relationship marketing and imaginary organizations: a synthesis. *European journal of Marketing*, 30(2), 31-44.

Payne, A. and Frow, P. (2005). A Strategic Framework for Customer Relationship Management. *Journal of Marketing*, 69 (4), 167-176.

Ryals, L. (2005). Making customer relationship management work: the measurement and profitable management of customer relationships. *Journal of Marketing*, 69(4), 252-261.

Saarijärvi, H., Karjaluoto, H., & Kuusela, H. (2013). Extending customer relationship management: from empowering firms to empowering customers.*Journal of Systems and Information Technology*, 15(2), 140-158.

Sheth, J. N, & Parvatiyar, A, (1995). The Evolution of Relationship Marketing. *International Business Review*, 4 (4), 397-418.

Teo, T. S., Devadoss, P., & Pan, S. L. (2006). Towards a holistic perspective of customer relationship management (CRM) implementation: A case study of the Housing and Development Board, Singapore. *Decision support systems*, 42(3), 1613-1627.

Vannin, M. (2004). Justifying CRM Costs and Boosting Return on Investment. Gartner Inc. available via http://pdf.aminer.org/000/304/390/analysis_of_costs_benefits_and_roi_of_crm_implementation.pdf

www.statehousing.com.gh/category/exhibition/

University of Ghana Access Control Project

Emmanuel Oware and Richard Boateng

> This case study is about how an African University created and used an access control system to solve a perennial heavy vehicular traffic problem. This decision triggered a public outcry and some protests from internal stakeholders while the government pressured the university to rescind its decision. The University Management stuck to their decision, navigating through all opposition including court suits to successfully implement and operationalise the access control system in support of its corporate objective of providing a serene learning and teaching environment.

Problem Context

Antecedents to the Access Control System

The University of Ghana is the premier and the largest public university in Ghana. Founded in 1948, the University's purpose is to provide and promote university education, learning, and research (UG, 2016). In a recent world university ranking of Times Higher Education, the university was ranked seventh in the whole of Africa, making it the topmost University in the West Africa sub-region (Amoa, 2016). This achievement is partly attributed to the university's current vision of becoming a world-class research-intensive university over the next decade. With the new strategic plan (2014-2024), the University aims to excel in research and make an impact at the national and international levels.

In line with its vision, the University seeks to provide a conducive environment for academic work at its campuses. It is in this light that the University Management decided to respond decisively to a perennial heavy vehicular traffic problem that had become a common feature on its main campus at Legon, in Accra. Motorists had been using the Legon campus as a thoroughfare from one end of town to the other. The unusual traffic on campus had affected the serene environment needed for learning. A survey report indicated that about 16,000 vehicles plied the university roads daily (GhanaCulturePolitics, 2014). As a result, students were contending with vehicles regarding their movement on campus. 'The situation poses danger to the lives of the students,' remarked one professor. Another remarked, 'the traffic is unbearable.' (GhanaCulturePolitics, 2014). One major concern expressed by the university community was the worsening condition of the roads on campus. Many sections of the road had developed potholes 'The road is too bad, we pay a lot and generally the roads in the school are bad,' said Joseph Aba, a level 400 Microbiology student' (Odetola, 2012).

In 2011, the idea to reduce the vehicular traffic and rehabilitate the roads was conceived. A feasibility study was conducted on how to manage the traffic situation on campus and to determine the cost of constructing and resurfacing the roads. On February 27, 2013, the University issued a public statement about its intention to undertake major road construction and rehabilitation works of some selected roads leading to and from the Legon main campus (GhanaCulturePolitics, 2014). The university contracted a bank loan facility of $2.3 million to enable it to achieve this objective. In order to repay the loan and fund the continued maintenance of the roads, the University Management decided to toll its roads to generate the needed revenue. The Ministry of Roads and Highways lauded this initiative in an opening ceremony (GhanaCulturePolitics, 2014).

The population of students is over 38,000 at the Legon campus, including international students from over 70 countries. The campus is about 13 kilometres northeast of the centre of Accra, the capital of Ghana, at an altitude of between 300 and 400 feet. The Legon campus has five entry/exit points:

1. **Main entrance:** The main entrance to the campus is directly opposite the main Legon police station at the north-eastern part of the campus. It leads into a major Accra-Dodowa dual carriage road. Within the period in focus, this entrance was closed to all motorists because it was under rehabilitation

2. **Okponglo entrance:** This entrance is along the same perimeter of the main entrance and leads into the Accra-Dodowa dual carriage road through a very busy traffic light junction. This traffic light is one source of traffic build-up on the Accra-Dodowa road. With the main entrance closed to traffic, this entrance served as the main entrance to the University.
3. **TF entrance:** This entrance is at the northern part of the campus. It leads into the heavily used Dome-North Legon road;
4. **Presec entrance:** This entrance is on the north-eastern part of campus and shares a perimeter with the main entrance leading into the Accra- Dodowa dual carriage road;
5. **Link gate entrance:** This entrance is on the southern part of campus. It leads into the Legon-Achimota road, another busy road.

It is evident that these five entry/exit points make the Legon campus a convenient thoroughfare for motorists.

The goal of the toll was to generate income while controlling access to the university. The strategy was to use an access control system. Since this was going to take time, it was decided to phase its implementation starting with daily tolls. On 1 February 2014, after the completion of a greater part of the resurfacing and construction of roads, the university started tolling the roads (Daily Graphic, 2014b) at the TF, Presec and Link gate entrances. Motorists were required to pay GH¢1 (US $ 0.4) for private and GH¢2-3 (US $0.8 – 1.2) for commercial vehicles at these entry points except the Okpanglo entrance. This action of the University triggered a public outcry because it created a heavy traffic build up in all connected roads to the university. The students who owned cars protested. There were also protests from parents who had to drop and pick up their children from the University's primary school, which is located on campus. The public protests mounted with accusations against the university authorities that they were going beyond their legal bounds. Some students went to the courts. The parents of the children at the primary school also took the university to court. However, the legal suits against the university failed and rather strengthened the University's resolve to determine who could access their premises. The unyielding position of the university's authorities in the midst of growing public agitation, led topressure from government ministries and various civil society groups to stop the tolls prompting an intervention by the Ghana National Security.

On 27 February 2015, three weeks after the university's measures, operatives from the National Security stormed the University of Ghana (Legon Campus) and demolished the toll booth structure under construction at the Okponglo entrance. This led to the temporary suspension of the tolls. However, the University Management rebounded back with a new directive instituting the use of UG (University of Ghana) car stickers to restrict access to the university's campus. The sticker was quite expensive at a price of GHc 400 (US $115) per year (in 2015). The intension was to deter the larger public from using the university as a thoroughfare. The UG sticker authorised users to use all the entry/exit points of the university. Those without stickers, who needed to come to the University of Ghana to conduct business (such as admission enquiries), were to come in and go out through the Okponglo entrance only. The University Management used the UG stickers to leverage their legal position - that the Legon campus was a private property and not a public one. The UG sticker helped to greatly restrict access to the university and this reduced traffic. However, the tolls triggered protests from the students and parents of wards of the University Primary School (UPS). A settlement was made with students to pay a processing fee for the sticker, while the parents had a 50% discount off the annual amount. The UG car sticker was subsequently replaced with the more effective access control system from October 2015.

Development and Implementation of UG Access Control System

Project Objectives

Every organisational information system has business and system objectives (Reich & Benbasat, 2000). The system objective should be aligned with the business objective. Given the background of the case, it is evident that the access control system (ACS) was part of an overall strategy of the university to achieve the following organisational objectives:

- To prevent the use of the Legon campus as a thorough fare by the public and to decongest it of the heavy vehicular traffic.
- To ensure that only people who had business with the University were allowed into the premises of the university.
- To generate revenue to fund maintenance of the roads.

The system's objective was to provide an automatic means for identifying and granting access to motorists coming into and leaving the campus.

System Design

This section looks at the design (i.e. the technical) aspect of the system. The ACS comprises mainly a front and a backend component. The front-end component controls incoming and outgoing vehicles at the entry/exist points of the university, while the backend component supports the administrative functions of the system, mainly the enrolment and issue of e-cards to the road users. The backend component comprises a computer server with an attached read-write card device. All data on registered vehicles are held on this server. The backend component is housed at the main entrance to the university, operated and managed by Angel Data and Telecoms Services, the outsourcing company. The front-end component is housed in the toll booths located at the entry/exit points to the university. A front-end component comprises the entry sensor, radio frequency identification (RFID) reader, personal computer controller (PC-controller), an external display, an exit sensor, camera, the barrier bar and traffic controller. The PC-controller holds a copy of the data held on the server. Data on newly issued cards are updated on each PC-controller at the toll booth in an offline mode within 24 hours. This could be done in real time if the server and PC-controller are linked. In the case of the university's system, they are not currently linked and therefore the need to update the PC-controllers with new e-card information within 24 hours in offline mode.

Each e-card issued to a user is encoded with a unique code. The code is linked to the license plate registration number of an enrolled vehicle as well as other details of the user. The e-card is held in a cardholder and fixed on the inside of the windscreen at the right corner. On approach of a vehicle from 50 meters away, the entry sensor detects the vehicle's entry and activates the RFID reader. The reader captures automatically the unique code of the e-card and starts the verification process while the vehicle stops at the red light signal of the traffic light controller within the entry loop of the toll booth. When the vehicle is successfully verified, the traffic light controller turns green and the barrier bar is raised to allow entry or exit. During the authentication process, the reader sends the e-card code to the PC-controller.

The PC-controller checks if the code belongs to the university and whether the date on the card is active (not expired). It retrieves the associated vehicle registration number from the database and displays it on the external display unit for the attention of the security officer. The officer will check the displayed vehicle number with that of the waiting vehicle. If all checks are valid, the bar is automatically lifted up for the vehicle to pass. As the vehicle leaves, the exit sensor senses the exit using the back tyre of the vehicle. The sensor sends the exit information to the barrier bar to come down. The whole process takes 1 to 3 mins. If it takes about 5 minutes, then there is a problem and the vehicle is made to pull over.

The camera is used for security purposes. It records incoming and outgoing vehicles to support investigation and incident reporting purposes. The system has a backup power supply - a 10 KVA UPS and generator.

System Development and Implementation

The university engaged the services of Angel Data and Telecoms Services (ADTS) as the external technical partner to supply, install, and manage the access control system (ACS). ADTS was selected because of their proven experience in implementing access control systems for corporate bodies and at the national level for the Ghana Highway Authority.

The management team for the project comprise the Registrar who was aided by an ad-hoc steering committee and the Physical Development and Municipal Services Directorate (PDMSD) of the university as the implementing unit. The Registrar who is the chief operating officer of the University chaired the ad-hoc steering committee meetings. The committee had representatives from the university's units, namely University of Ghana Computer Systems (UGCS), Internal Audit, Finance, Legal Counsel, Security, and the PDMSD. Also included on the committee were representatives from the student body and GPRTU. Other members were co-opted as needed. Committee meetings were held to vet the contract with ADTS, discuss the likely implementation challenges and policy. Emergent issues were discussed.

One major policy approved by the University Management was a minimum number of free e-card allocations to the various categories of staff. Under the policy, senior staff and lecturers on contract are entitled to two free e-cards. The junior staff, part-time lecturers, pensioners are entitled to one free e-card. Staff who require additional e-cards will purchase the e-card just as any road user. After protests from students, they were persuaded to pay GH¢50 annually as processing fee for the e-card. The stakeholder parents reluctantly were asked to pay for e-cards at a 50% discount.

During the implementation, the PDMSD coordinated the construction of the physical structures required to operate the ACS at the entry points of the University.

The physical structures included the construction and resurfacing of the roads, construction of and power supply to the toll booths. The in-house professional staff of the PDMSD, comprising architects, quantity surveyors, draughtsmen, and electrical technicians worked with a contracted construction firm to construct the roads and structures. These tasks were executed as part of their normal work processes where work orders were raised and executed. Therefore, there was no dedicated team assigned to this project. Meetings were held as and when necessary. After the delivery of the ACS, the PDMSD exercised the administrative role by liaising with the ADTS for processing applications and issue of e-cards for internal stakeholders.

According to ADTS, the ACS was implemented at the Presec, TF and Link-gate entrances within two months from May to July 2015 soon after the booth infrastructure had been provided. There was a trial run, which lasted up to October 2015. The ACS was operationally effective at these three entrances from October 2015. The ACS at the main gate entrance was installed much later in April 2016. The ACS for the Okponglo entrance remains.

The UG stickers were used in conjunction with the ACS until they were phased out. Some initial problems with the ACS such as the barrier bar not lifting up as expected and the long wait at the toll booth were encountered but resolved. With the commissioning of the ACS, vehicular access to the campus was effectively restricted. Motorists were required to purchase an e-Card to be able to go through the University. The ACS resolved the problems with the UG sticker such as duplication and manipulation by the officers in charge and the road users.

System Operations

The process for acquiring e-cards is segmented according to user type, i.e. staff, students, and the public.

For staff, e-card acquisition is made through the PDMSD based on the free e-card allocation policy. As a control mechanism, staff members' identities are authenticated using their unique staff numbers. This is extracted along with staff details from the University's corporate HR database onto an Excel sheet maintained by the PDMSD. In addition, staff members are required to provide vehicle roadworthy certificates. The certificate serves two purposes. First, is to establish the true ownership of the vehicle and to prevent staff from registering vehicles for others. Second, is to determine if the vehicle is commercial or private. The policy does not allocate free e-cards for staff who had commercial vehicles. The Excel worksheet is updated with vehicle information and a list generated with a cover letter to ADTS to produce the e-cards. The PDMSD receive completed e-cards, sort and distribute them to staff.

For students, the procedure is to write to the Dean of Students office for permission for the issue of e-card. Enclosed in the letter is a road-worthy certificate and evidence of being a student using admission letter, student ID card or registration certificate. The Dean of Students will authenticate the status of the applicant as a student based on the University's school management system. A letter is written to ADTS through the PDMSD authorising the issue of the e-card to the student. Students are only required to pay GH¢50 as processing fee for the e-card.

For the public, the procedure is to purchase the e-card directly from ADTS. As of June 2016, the payment rates for the private vehicles were: GH¢400 (US $100) per year; GH¢250 (US $62.5) per half-year and GH¢150 (US $37.5) per quarter. For commercial vehicles it is GH¢500 (US $125) per year.

The usage policy is one card to a vehicle. If a valid card is used with an unregistered car, the security officer may notice it. As indicated in the system design, the ACS will display the vehicle registration number based on the unique code of the vehicle. It is then left to the human attendant to make the match. This is one weakness of the system. Problem users are cautioned and finally blacklisted if they continue to be difficult. ADTS generates monthly reports on transactions, financials, and incidences for the University Management. According to ADTS, the operational challenges that have been encountered include unstable power supply, difficulties with some uncooperative users, as well as some who do not understand how the system works. According to the ADTS, the vehicular traffic on campus has been reduced approximately by half.

Factors which shaped the Project

To facilitate the analysis of the case, McLeod & MacDonel's (2011) four dimension factor-model will be adapted. They are institutional, project, people and development process.

Institutional, Development, People and Dimensions

The actors in the case were the University Management, government, staff, students, stakeholder parents, and the public. Given this complex array of stakeholders, how was the university able to push through an access policy, which involved tolling university roads that for many years had been used as a thoroughfare? Did they have the powers to do it? In information systems development (ISD), power, politics, and resistance characterise systems implementation and therefore implementers should be aware of their influence (Markus & Keil, 1994).

The university derives its powers from the Act (i.e. Act 79 in 1961 amended as Act 2010). The Act establishes the university as an autonomous institution though it is a public one. The Supreme Court of Ghana affirmed the university's autonomy and rights to do as it sees fit with its premises following a petition brought before it by some students (Djabanor, 2015). The decision to toll the roads was sanctioned by the university's Council, the highest decision making body in the university. The Council includes five representatives appointed by the President of Ghana with one of them being the Chairperson of the Council. In addition, the Ministry of Roads and Highways publicly supported the initiative to toll the roads. These factors confirm that the government did not have issues with the decision to toll the roads. However, following the backlash from the public, the government backtracked asking the University to rescind its decision (Daily Graphic, 2014a). The University Management did not give in to pressure from the government and other influential groups such as diplomats even after the demolition by the National Security operatives.

With respect to the internal environment, the authorities had to deal with initial resistance by staff, students, and stakeholder parents of the wards at the University's primary school who did not see why they should be made to pay for the use of the roads. The allocation policy of e-cards and persuasion of the student body to accept the processing fee helped to diffuse resistance from these internal stakeholders. Handling of the parent's issue was an afterthought. In the end, it was a 'win-win' situation unlike in some systems implementations where one-user group gains power at the expense of others (Robey & Markus, 1994).

One thing that clearly stands out is the resilience showed by the University Management. This played a major role in the success of the project, though there were shortcomings with the university's engagement with the public. All the interviewed participants agreed the engagement with the public could have been done better:

'We couldn't have anticipated such an act by the National security but I believe if we had done some effective education with the public it could have been prevented' (UG ACS Operations Officer)

> *'The standoff with the parents could have been avoided. Although the University won the court proceeding, it affected the objective since at some point the parents blocked the road and restricted people from coming in'*
> (Project Implementing Team Member at PDMSD)

> *The university of Ghana project was quite different from other implementations considering acceptance. Asking staff and students to pay for the use of roads was an issue. Education would have helped.*
> (ADTS Project Manager)

The university authorities engaged the public on various platforms, but as events showed it was not adequate.

Project Content and Development Process

In ISD, one of the factors that leads to failed IS projects is unclear project goals and objectives (Ewusi-Mensah, 1997). The UG access control system had clear project objectives and scope and they were aligned to management's goals. The university's community shared in it, though the student body and staff at some point were not happy with the implementation. The adhoc steering committee had representations from stakeholders – except the parents.

The technical aspect of the development and execution was almost without problems. As the PM of the ADTS remarked:

> *'The problems we had was not technical but there was an issue with who bears the cost of repairs and profit sharing. The reaction of the university community to the system was quite different from our experience with other implementations'*

This observation is consistent with ISD literature that systems implementations are different because of different contexts in which they are implemented (Avgerou, 2000). Secondly, most problems in systems development are largely people-related (Doherty & King, 1998; Markus & Keil, 1994).

Discussion and Conclusion

The development and implementation of the ACS at the university was characterised by clash of interests, power, and competence. Clash of interests because of the varied stakeholders. The display of powers – external pressure from the public, the government, and protests from internal stakeholders - staff, students, and parents against the University Management. It is evident that the resilience of the University Management paid off though at some costs such as the demolition of an uncompleted toll booth. In ISD, top management commitment is widely acknowledged as a key success factor in IS projects (Ewusi-Mensah, 1997; McLeod & MacDonell, 2011).

The case study has given rich insight into the dynamics of top management commitment as a success factor in ISD. The new insight is resilience of top management, which is being used here to refer to commitment backed by power. A management may be committed but without the legal power base, they may not be able to push through their objectives as evidenced by this case. If the Supreme Court had ruled against the University Management, it would have significantly affected the project despite the commitment of management. The resilience of the University Management is demonstrated by two bold moves. First, the decision to contract a $2.3m loan, which is a novelty for a public university in Ghana. Second, instituting tolls on roads that had been used by the public for many years and not backing down despite government pressures and intimidation, and competently dealing with stakeholder resistance.

Indications are that the University Management and stakeholders are satisfied with the project outcomes. The university's campus has significantly been rid of vehicular traffic with new-asphalted roads and funds to maintain them. Considering that the set objectives of the University were achieved the project has arguably been a success.

Questions

1. The actors and their actions in the ISD process characterise the human-side issues. Identify these actors and explain how their interests and therefore actions affected the project.
2. What were the major stages or events that characterised the projects?
3. The University Management's resilience helped greatly to achieve success of the project. Explain how and what is your comment considering the project's outcome in respect of its objectives?

References

Amoa, S. (2016). News Release: University of Ghana Hits 7th Position of Best Universities in Africa. Retrieved June 3, 2016, from http://www.ug.edu.gh/news/news-release-university-ghana-hits-7th-position-best-universities-africa

Avison, D., & Fitzgerald, G. (2003). Where now for development methodologies? *Communications of the ACM, 46*(1), 78–82.

Bansler, J., & Damsgaard, J. (2000). Corporate intranet implementation: managing emergent technologies and organizational practices. *Journal of the Association for Information Systems*.

Brewer, G., Neubauer, B., & Geiselhart, K. (2006). Designing and Implementing E-Government Systems Critical Implications for Public Administration and Democracy. *Administration & Society, 38*(4), 472–499.

Burrell, G., & Morgan, G. (1979). *Sociological paradigms and organisational analysis* (Vol. 248). london: Heinemann.

Daily Graphic. (2014a). Rescind Decision On Tolls - Government Urges Legon. Retrieved May 24, 2016, from http://www.peacefmonline.com/pages/local/news/201402/189100.php

Daily Graphic. (2014b). University of Ghana defends road tolls. Retrieved June 3, 2016, from http://www.graphic.com.gh/news/general-news/17532-university-of-ghana-defends-road-tolls.html

Djabanor, F. (2015). Supreme Court dismisses road toll petition against Legon. Retrieved May 30, 2016, from http://citifmonline.com/2015/07/16/supreme-court-dismisses-road-toll-case-against-legon/

Doherty, N., & King, M. (1998). The consideration of organizational issues during the systems development process: an empirical analysis. *Behaviour & Information Technology*.

Ewusi-Mensah, K. (1997). Critical issues in abandoned information systems development projects. *Communications of the ACM*.

GhanaCulturePolitics. (2014). *DOCUMENTARY: PUBLIC Access to University of Ghana roads*. Ghana. Retrieved from https://www.youtube.com/watch?v=0GAUwNJLEW0

Hastie, S., & Wojewoda, S. (2015). Standish Group 2015 Chaos Report - Q&A with Jennifer Lynch. Retrieved May 22, 2016, from https://www.infoq.com/articles/standish-chaos-2015

Markus, L., & Keil, M. (1994). If We Build It, They Will Come: Designing Information Systems that People Want to Use. *Sloan Management Review*, 35(4), 11–25.

Markus, M. (1983). Power, politics, and MIS implementation. *Communications of the ACM*, 26(6), 430–444.

McLeod, L., & Doolin, B. (2012). Information systems development as situated socio-technical change: a process approach. *European Journal of Information* ....

McLeod, L., & MacDonell, S. (2011). Factors that affect software systems development project outcomes: A survey of research. *ACM Computing Surveys (CSUR)*.

Newman, M., & Robey, D. (1992). A Social Process Model of User-Analyst Relationships. *MIS Quarterly*, 16(2), 249–266.

Odetola, O. (2012). Pot Holes in University of Ghana Campus. Retrieved June 1, 2016, from https://thescsbeat.wordpress.com/2012/11/26/pot-holes-in-university-of-ghana-campus/

Reich, B. H. B., & Benbasat, I. (2000). Factors that influence the social dimension of alignment between business and information technology objectives. *MIS Quarterly*, 24(1), 81–113. http://doi.org/10.2307/3250980

Robey, D., & Markus, M. (1984). Rituals in information system design. *MIS Quarterly*, 8(1), 5–15.

Sarker, S. (2000). Toward a methodology for managing information systems implementation: A social constructivist perspective. *Informing Science*.

UG. (2016). UG Overview. Retrieved June 3, 2016, from http://www.ug.edu.gh/about/overview

Bank Customer Service Concerns in BF Bank of Ghana

Ibn Kailan Abdul-Hamid

> BF Bank of Ghana is among the very first banks to have started the banking business in Ghana. This case mirrors a possible linkage of a bank branch manager losing his job for not delivering good client services to BF clients that bank with his branch. The case also argues for the need for managers to be customer service champions.

Firm Information

BF Bank is a leading financial services provider with over 97 years of banking experience in Ghana and a well-established local presence (http://gh.bf.com). BF Ghana is a member of the BF Africa Group Limited (BAGL), which is majority-owned by BF Bank PLC. BF Africa Group Limited is one of Africa's major financial services institutions offering personal and business banking, credit cards, corporate & Investment banking and wealth management products and services as well as bancassurance. BF Bank combines global expertise and product knowledge with the rich experience and appreciation of the local environment to bring the best of banking to our people like no other. BF has 75 service outlets nationwide: 57 branches, 3 Agencies, 10 Prestige Centres and 2 Premier Suites.

BF Ghana also has over 155 ATMs spread across the country. In addition to these, there is an array of free e-banking solutions (Internet Banking, Hello Money - Mobile

Banking, Smartphone Banking, SMS Alerts and e-Statements) which customers can access any time of the day. Corporate & Treasury products are targeted particularly at business and corporate clients, while they extend Business Banking products and services to Small & Medium Scale Enterprises and indigenous businesses. The Retail function has a three-tier personal banking proposition (Personal, Prestige & Premier) for individual customers. All Retail customers enjoy free access to their range of e-banking solutions. Corporate clients can also use the BF Integrator (our online banking application for corporate customers) to manage their corporate transactions from wherever they are.

BF offers you a whole range of options that will enable you to enjoy banking services wherever and whenever you need to. With just your mobile phone, laptop, tablet or PC, you can access your accounts and transact anytime, using Internet Banking, Hello Money - Mobile Banking, Smartphone Banking, SMS Alerts and e-Statements. BF e-banking platforms are secure, fast, convenient and reliable, so you can do your banking when it suits you - 24 hours a day, 7 days a week. The e-banking services are free.

BF continues to support the development and growth of the local economy through cocoa syndication and financing. BF was also one of the lead managers for Ghana's second Eurobond, which was issued in July 2013, to raise US$1 billion for the government of Ghana. BF is committed to investing its resources, including employee time and expertise in community programmes to enhance the employability, enterprise and financial literacy skills of the youth – the next generation.

Recent Innovations

Recent innovations in BF include:

1. CashSend, a new and convenient money transfer service, which allows customers to send or receive cash at any BF ATM within Ghana. The receiver need not be a customer nor have an account with the bank.
2. Cash-accepting ATMs, where an Intelligent ATMs allow customers to make deposits anytime of the day at their convenience.
3. BF Bank offers free Credit life by paying for the cost of insurance on unsecured loans. Now loan repayments are lower each month while customers still enjoy the benefits of insurance.

4. Ping It is a smart, convenient, hassle-free and secure banking solution for receiving remittances from the UK.
5. Negotiable Certificate of Deposit (NCD) is an exciting new fixed interest investment instrument and the first in Ghana's financial market. NCD buyers can invest for 91 days, 182 days, 270 days or 365 days and earn higher interest than what they would earn on existing government instruments of equivalent tenures.
6. Risk Management Solutions is designed to help clients reduce or eliminate their risks in the areas of foreign exchange, interest rate and commodity prices. Options, Swaps and Forward contracts have been introduced.

In 2014, BF Bank of Ghana was named the Best Bank in Ghana by Euromoney. Receiving the award, the BF Ghana Managing Director, Patience, said the recognition was a testimony of the strides the bank was making towards the goal of becoming the bank of choice by delivering better value banking to the Ghana market. Shortly after rejoicing for wining an international award, Kweku got an email from his manager expelling him with effect from December, 2015. This was a result of his failure to improve customer service at his branch, because customer service is clearly very important to BF Bank.

Although BF Bank staff have undergone periodic training on customer service to enhance their customer service skills, the level of customer service delivery at Kweku's branch was very poor. As a result of the continual entry of new banks into the Ghanaian banking sector, BF Bank cannot rest on its oars. BF is poised to maintain and improve on its market share in Ghana. Kweku also mentioned that BF Bank customers are topmost in preference in service delivery. BF customers need services to be delivered to them fast. Subsequently, BF clients wish to be treated nicely and welcomed to the banking halls. Finally, customers complain that BF staff (at Kweku's branch) are not well educated on the bank's services.

The decision to sack Kweku was based on a customer service report on his branch. A survey of BF's customers at his branch revealed the following:

After running two accounts with BF for 8 Years, I went to buy a draft for my brother's school admission fee. Apart from waiting for about 30 minutes, the front desk officer at BF mentioned that the transaction was not approved. Hence, I had to go to another bank because the name was flagged in their systems, attempts to get the officers to approve the transaction was not yielding any results.

I went to deposit money at a branch of BF Bank. The IT system was down and customers were not notified. We waited for hours until after visibly showing our frustration I left.

I had a student account when I was on Legon campus. After graduating, I made attempts to update my records but all fell on deaf ears. After six months, anytime I went to withdraw money, the bank staff will ask me why I was still using a students' account. Their problem was that even though it was a savings account, I could withdraw everything in the account. The bank authorities kept asking me the same question several times. I stopped using that bank because I felt they should be answering the question instead.

I had a standing order with BF Bank to pay my insurers GHC100 every month. After three years I went to my insurers to check my account only to be told that my bankers had not paid although they deducted Ghc100 from my account for three years. When I drew their attention, it took them another six whole months to correct it.

I went to BF Legon to cash a BF Osu Branch cheque. After being in the queue for more than 30 minutes, the teller told me I can only cash at Achimota since it is a third party cheque. I insisted to pick the proceeds from Osu since they pride themselves as a branch network. I was asked to step aside for the next person to be served. I refused and eventually the operations manager authorized that the cheque be honoured.

BF Bank High street will call to confirm a cheque which had been issued to a 3rd party. I missed their call but called back to confirm the cheque. The officer who picked the phone said he was not the one who called so he couldn't help me and would not take my explanation.

I have two accounts with BF Bank, a current and savings account. I took a loan from the bank and was servicing it with the current accounts. I walked into the bank one afternoon to pay money into the current account only to be told that the account had been closed. I was told that it was an internal error which should be rectified *very soon. I had to therefore deposit the money into the savings account. A month later, I had a call from the bank that I had defaulted in servicing the loan. I went to the Bank and informed the Customer Service manager that the bank would have to reactivate my current account so that I can conveniently service the loan. In the interim however, deductions could be made from my savings account. I was told that using my savings account to service the loan was not possible and that whilst I wait for the re-activation of the current account. I should service the loan by direct payment into a special account of the bank.*

As part of the report on Kweku's branch customer service delivery, the following arguments were reechoed as benefits BF Bank had missed for not engaging in delivering customer service.

Customer service is the service provided in support of a company's core products. Customer service can occur on-site (that is, when a retail employee helps a customer to find a desired item or answers a question for example) or it can occur over the phone or via the Internet (Hinson, 2012). Quality customer service is the key element required for a successful bank. Satisfactory response from consumers means increased sales, which ultimately leads to increased satisfaction of shareholders. They tend to invest more in your organization, which can dramatically improve the Return on Investment (ROI) of your business. Also, quality service can boost BF Bank's growth. Quality services could help BF expand its client base but great customer service is the key to retain your clients and stand out of the crowd.

BF Bank should encourage consumers to provide feedback and comments, as it is an integral part of quality customer service. It is probably the best way to understand the expectations of customers and adopt successful business strategies. Customer service can provide BF a critical learning experience to understand the dynamics of the corporate world. Understating the expectations and mindset of customers can considerably reduce the risk of BF Bank losses. As Hinson (2012) notes 'Quality customer service is essential to building customer relationships. It should, however, not be confused with the service provided for sale by the company'.

Kweku argued that when customers are happy, BF's investors and business partners will be happy as well. This ultimately leads to higher profits. With a strong client base we can win the trust of investors and make the most of every viable business opportunity. With increased sales and higher profits, you can offer employees good salary packages and additional bonuses, thus reducing employee turnover. Also, client satisfaction directly influences the working environment of business organizations.

With decreased pressure of meeting targets and financial stability, employees can work in a comfortable corporate atmosphere, thus encouraging them to work to their maximum capacity.

In conclusion, technology was noted as a tool for facilitating basic customer service functions (bill paying, checking account records, tracking orders), transactions (both retail and business-to business) and information seeking. Technology also facilitates transactions by offering a direct vehicle for making purchases and conducting business. As Internet banking grows worldwide, banks like BF should enhance their technology delivering client services like: Internet banking and Mobile banking.

Questions

1. What are the benefits of delivering customer service to bank clients?
2. What can happen to a manager or employee who fails to deliver customer service?
3. How can customer service delivery enhance the competitiveness of a bank?

References
Hinson, R.E (2012). *Services Marketing with a Twist of Corporate Social Responsibility.* Sedco publishing, Accra Ghana.

Hinson, R.E. (2016). *Customer Service Essentials.* Centre for Sustainability and Enterprise Development and Centre for Business Dynamics. Accra, Ghana and South Africa.

Developing E-commerce Capabilities in a Beverage Manufacturing Firm

Richard Boateng

> This case study explores how a beverage manufacturing firm in Ghana orients resources to develop capabilities which achieve value through electronic commerce.

Kasadrin Company Limited - Firm Profile

Kasadrin Company Limited (KCL) was incorporated on March, 1987 after it had begun operations as a small-scale manufacturer of alcoholic and non-alcoholic beverages in 1986. The company focuses on producing alcoholic and non-alcoholic beverages to satisfy consumers, primarily in Ghana. KCL has 13 products. The company's indigenous products are Opeimu Bitters, Alomo Bitters, Alomo Root Wine, Kasadrin Dry Gin, Kasadrin Brandy, Kasadrin Tonic Wine, Kasapak, Cream Soda Mix, Lime Cordial, and Aperitif Sherry Red Wine. The other three products, Three Barrels Brandy, Pixie Dry Gin and Flavoured Cardinal Liqueurs, are produced by the company under license from a Dutch alcohol manufacturer. KCL's major products, or as termed 'flagship' products, are Alomo Bitters and Alomo Root Wine. Its indigenous products are developed through research-collaboration with the Centre for Scientific Research into Plant Medicine (CSRPM), Ghana.

The raw materials for the other products and other related materials for production are sourced both locally and internationally. Local sourcing is done by telephone and email and international or foreign sourcing is done electronically through the Internet and email, supported by telephone communication and frequent visits. Flavours are obtained from France, metal and plastic caps from India, plastic laminates for pouch making/filling from India and glass bottles from Germany. Alcohol is supplied by another Ghanaian company which imports it from different countries including Brazil. The firm also uses the Internet to find information on how to maintain production machinery and source for spare parts from machine building companies in Germany.

Through an intra-organisational network system, the bottling and plant department is informed of the type and quantity of the product to be produced daily. The concentrates for the products are prepared and placed in the automated bottling processor. The respective bottles or sachets of the product are placed in the automated bottling processor consisting of four main stages; washing, filling, labelling and packaging. During these processes the products are regularly inspected by the quality assurance unit to identify bottles with low fills, bad capping/uncapped bottles, bottles with cracks from movement in the automated processor and bottles with twisted labels or wrong labels. Packaged products are placed into storage for distribution. After payments are made for product orders, the sales and marketing manager authorises goods to be delivered to distributors or individuals who are buying in large quantities, usually for an event. The firm distributes an average of 3,000,000 cartons of its products annually through a network of over 50 distributors.

KCL has three executive directors, who run the company with the support of seven managers who form the management team. The three executive directors consist of executive chairman, executive director and the managing director, who is also the founder of the company. The managing director (MD) is a graduate of EMPRETEC Ghana, an UNCTAD capacity-building programme for SMEs and entrepreneurial skills promotion. He is also an executive member of the Chartered Institute of Administration of Ghana. The executive chairman holds a PhD in agricultural economics and is a fellow of the Chartered Institute of Bankers (Ghana). The executive director has a bachelor's degree in electrical and electronic engineering and master's in business administration. KCL's executives are supported by a management team consisting of sales and marketing manager, bottling and plant manager, general manager for finance and accounting, purchasing and supply manager, marketing and public relations manager, general manager for operations, and information systems manager. These managers have postgraduate degrees and professional qualifications related to their respective managerial functions. The IT unit is made up of the IS manager and an IT technician. The IT unit is responsible for all IS-related issues. KCL has a permanent workforce of 101 who work in unison with approximately between 150 and 180 casual labourers yearly.

KCL has 30 workstations ranging from Pentium III to Pentium IV computers, connected to a network at the rate of 100Mbps. The firm obtained its first Internet subscription in 2001. It currently subscribes to a broadband Internet service from a local ISP – a speed of 512kps at a cost of US$120 a month. As a company policy, only the workstations of the executive, managers and secretaries have access to the Internet. KCL's email system is hosted by a local firm, CT Solutions, which also developed and hosts the company's website. For the procurement and management of the company's IT infrastructure and business systems, the company manages close working relationships with four trading partners, including CT Solutions.

KCL has been a member of the Ghana Club 100 since 2002. The Ghana Club 100 ranked the firm tenth in the manufacturing industry in 2003, and named the firm the second most profitable Ghanaian company in 2004, with a return on equity of 134 percent. In the overall rankings of the top 100 companies in Ghana, the firm placed sixteen in 2003; fifteen in 2004, and nine in 2005 (Ghana Club 100, 2004, 2005). Exhibit 7 shows the financial profile of KCL.

	2001	2002	2004	2005
Turnover (US Dollars)	672,050	4.7 million	18.6 million	14.2 million
Net Profit After Tax (US Dollars)			3.1 million	4.4 million
Employee Size (Permanent Workforce)	101	101	101	101

Source: KCL Facts Sheet (2006) and Ghana Club 100 (2004; 2005)

Exhibit 7 Financial Profile of Kasadrin Company Limited

Business Resource Development

Business Start-Up

KCL began as a small-scale alcoholic beverage-manufacturing firm in the home of the MD in 1986. As at that time, alcoholic beverage production was dominated by foreign imports and products of two large Ghanaian manufacturers and about a hundred family-oriented small-scale (in-house) manufacturers located in Nungua, a suburb of Accra. Though, as compared to foreign imports, the quality of locally brewed alcohol by small-scale manufacturers was relatively lower, they received an appreciable patronage. Foreign imports were expensive and the production volume of the Ghanaian manufacturers could not satisfy the demand. As a result, there was a growing demand for good quality alcoholic drinks that were relatively affordable to the average Ghanaian. This market niche inspired the MD to start the company. According to the MD,

> 'This insight was unique; ...we identified the increasing sophistication of the consumer. High expectations in terms of taste, quality, safety and packaging meant that the Ghanaian consumer was spending more on foreign imports that met their aspiration'.

The MD began the firm with three other close relations which included an ex-distillery worker who managed the production and two supporting staff for production and distribution. The MD was responsible for scouting customers, marketing, promoting and obtaining feedback from local drinking pubs. The number of employees became five when another friend joined the firm as the operations manager (also the current general manager for operations), managing daily operations of the firm, and doubling as the driver since he was the most knowledgeable about the capital city, Accra.

The first product was Kasadrin Gin. The name Kasadrin (pseudonym) was the appellation of a local chief in the Western region of Ghana (the MD's hometown). Kasadrin Gin became one of first locally named brands which were professionally packaged. Having an indigenous product which could match up to imported products was a potential sales and marketing factor for the company. KCL produced a total output of four cartons (64 litres) of Kasadrin gin per week. On his first day of doubling as a driver, the operations manager (OM) realised a caveat in the sales and marketing strategy. The company was selling and marketing its products during the normal working hours (8.00am to 5.00pm). However, within these times the owners of the bars and other public drinking places, who were primarily civil servants, were usually not available to make purchase decisions. This affected the sales of their products. Upon further discussions with the MD, it was decided that sales and marketing team change their working hours to the evening. The change gave the firm the opportunity to meet owners and part of the drinking community and introduce them to their products. The OM reflects that,

> 'The response was remarkable. Within one week, the company for its first time sold 20 cartons of Kasadrin Gin. For the owners of the public drinking places this was a welcome change in their operations; Kasadrin was serving them at their doorsteps, as compared to going to the established brewery companies and importers to purchase their products. As a new company with new brands of drinks this was the best option available to effectively market our products'.

Further, the local drinking pubs and alcoholic beverage retailers were also losing revenue from long waiting periods after making deposits to purchase imported products. Kasadrin therefore did not just offer a competing new brand, 'but became the readily available drink' (Interview with Nungua Local Resident (since 1987), AX Enterprise, 18 November, 2006). After a year, the company bought another van for sales, marketing and distribution. The MD and OM recruited new staff and trained them to manage the sales, marketing and distribution. On appointment, the new sales and marketing manager made another observation concerning the public advertisement of alcoholic products. The sales and marketing manager comments that,

> '...because of tax evasion some Ghanaian firms stayed away from public adverts, however, Kasadrin saw this as an opportunity and actively engaged in the public advertisement of their products. This increased the patronage of our products'.

As a registered company which adhered to tax responsibilities, KCL began to publicly advertise its products through the local media. This gave KCL some competitive edge over the other small-scale manufacturers which avoided such marketing opportunities. A tax officer at the Ghana VAT office confirmed that as part of the strategies for curbing tax evasion, the local media is monitored consistently to identify firms who are not listed in their databases. She notes that, 'It is very common to find many small businesses avoiding public advertisement in the local media because of tax issues.

These firms also avoid trade exhibitions. Though these are opportunities of expanding their market reach, they do not want their activities to be monitored by tax agencies or officials in Ghana' (Interview with Tax Officer, Ghana VAT Office, 4 December 2006). Additionally, the MD also introduced sales commissions and awards for meeting targets, which increased the commitment of the sales and marketing team, encouraging them to sell more of the products. The employees received commission on meeting sales targets and an extra commission for each sale beyond the sales target.

In the 1990's KCL focused on two major projects;

- Collaborating with CSPRM to explore the development of products from alcoholic extracts from traditional plants. Two products, Alomo Bitters and Alomo Root Wine, were introduced in 1999. The Alomo Bitters brand was awarded the Chartered Institute of Marketing, Ghana (CIMG) Product of the Year 1999 Award. The success of the collaboration between KCL and CSRPM also led to the research and development of Opeimu Bitters in 2005.
- Building an automated production factory with an administrative office block. The firm moved into the new factory premises in 2000 and the building was commissioned in 2001.

Thereafter, KCL changed its strategy from production, distribution and marketing to focus on their core objective of producing alcoholic and non-alcoholic beverages in 2003. Two issues necessitated the change in strategy. First, there was growing competition from foreign liquor and local manufacturers. A number of companies, including the local subsidiary of an international brewery company, had developed substitute products with indigenous Ghanaian names. Hence, the product and marketing strategy of KCL had been partly imitated. Second, the sales and marketing activities needed to go beyond Accra and the Southern sector of Ghana to the Northern sector. The Northern sector contributed only about one percent of the company's total sales. As a result, the firm changed its strategy to focus on production while supporting the distributors, who did the sales of products, with marketing and promotion.

The competitive strategy of KCL's competitors connotes with the Resource Based Theory's argument of creating substitute products to compete with that of the seeming successful firm. In this case, competing firms understood that creating socio-cultural connotation and relationships around their products was necessary to compete with the products of KCL. The general manager for finance and accounting (GFA) explains that, though KCL's net profit after tax increased by 42 percent in 2005, competition from foreign liquor and local producers made the industry very competitive leading to the decline in turn-over by 31 percent as compared to that of 2004.

Exploring Export Opportunities

In 2004, the firm began to receive distributorship and purchase enquiries via email and telephone from potential customers from other countries in West Africa, Europe and the USA. These enquiries were usually from Ghanaians who operated African or Ghanaian shops, drinking avenues and restaurants. The products usually requested for exports were Alomo Bitters and Opeimu Bitters. However, as of that time, the firm had no official organisational strategy to export outside the country. Products had usually been purchased and exported by Ghanaians living abroad and other foreigners at their own cost and usually for personal use. This was usually in small quantities and done with distributors, without the collaboration of the firm. Contributory reasons for the lack of an organisational export strategy were the untapped opportunities in Northern Ghana and the existence of a number of process issues within export trade. These process issues refer to meeting export-trade requirements and expectations of the export market while keeping the originality of the product. The sales and marketing manager comments that,

> 'The Internet has done its work in broadening the market, however there are key issues related to the import of alcoholic beverages which differs across the various countries. For example, the European Union had certain standards for importing alcoholic beverages especially in relation to alcohol levels. These products and related trading requirements are partly the issues stalling the exports of our brands'.

The failure to meet diverse export and product standards of developed countries has been argued as one of the major challenges of developing country (DC) firms, and may therefore affect their ability to increase their market reach through the Internet (Todaro and Smith, 2003: 575; Molla *et al.*, 2006b). Though the Internet had aided in initiating export trade enquiries through information on the firm's website and email communication, it was not enough to facilitate the export process. In 2005, KCL shipped two forty-foot containers, approximately 5000 cartons of Alomo Bitters to the USA after meeting a number of export trade requirements. This was a result of an email request by an interested customer to be sold in African shops and drinking places. In order to facilitate this order, the customer was referred to a US firm which was partly owned by the managing director of KCL. The US firm became the liaison between the customer and KCL; enabling KCL to acquire the necessary certification and facilitating pre- and post-contractual agreements. In the marketing manager's assessment,

> 'The customer was relatively determined to work with KCL through all the procedural stages in meeting all requirements and obtaining all the licenses required to export the products. The process is usually detailed and could take a number of months; some potential customers become disinterested as it becomes more costly in terms of time and resources'.

Extant literature shows that the lack of commitment, trust and compliance mechanisms affects decision-making and contributes to the loss of contracts and contractual disputes in transactions in the marketplace (Pare, 2003). Hence, the provision of the requisite measures to motivate actors participating in online transactions becomes critical. After realising the potential of the US market, KCL commissioned sales agents with sample products to study the foreign markets, specifically USA, Europe and West Africa in 2006. A primary issue indicated by the studies in the USA and Europe relates to the differences in product packaging across countries/regions. For example, in the USA market, customers found the long and big bottles of Alomo Bitters uncomfortable, since they were more accustomed to buying from the shelves and drinking from the bottle. The customers preferred the smaller bottles which they could easily carry and take sips from. In the European Union market, there was a preference for PET (Polyethylene Terephthalate) bottles, which are very lightweight, and more technically and practically recyclable as compared to glass bottles.

In West Africa, KCL identified a potential market for its products in countries which have had their nationals living in Ghana for a period by virtue of war and trade. Some of these nationals had experienced their products and were back in their countries. KCL decided to focus on recruiting distributors in these countries. KCL commissioned two sales representatives, one to work in francophone countries; Ivory Coast and Togo, and the other to work in Nigeria, Liberia, and Sierra Leone. The credibility of a prospective distributor was to be established through letters of credit through KCL's bankers and information from the trade missions of the countries involved. As of July 2007, two prospective distributors from Liberia and Nigeria had visited KCL to ascertain its production capacity in meeting their requirements before making a substantial investment in exports and distribution. These business considerations are yet to turn into transactions of financial value. Communication between the firm and the sales representatives has been supported by emails and telephone.

E-commerce Capabilities Development

The development of e-commerce capabilities in KCL can be traced in two main stages of developing informational and interactional e-commerce capabilities.

Informational E-commerce Capability (Jan 2001 – Dec 2001)

The firm considered building an informational e-commerce capability after adopting a connected form of e-commerce. The MD and the other firm managers had begun to use the Internet as a medium for sourcing production materials and equipment suppliers. Email was used to initiate business relationships with these suppliers and support transactions and negotiations with other trading partners in Europe and India. The firm had no IT manager. Internet access was being obtained from local cybercafés and this was not convenient, timely or efficient for the firm's productivity. The objective of the firm at this stage was to connect to the Internet and to create an online presence. The MD signed up for a dial-up package with a local ISP. The operations manager reflects that,

> 'At that time we only had two PCs, one used by the MD and another, shared by the rest of the managers. Only the MD's computer was connected to the Internet. To send an email you had to go to the MD's office and when you receive your emails, you either download them onto diskette or print them out directly'.

It was during this regular use of the Internet that they considered the Internet as a potential channel relevant for marketing and promotional activities. As most of the firm's foreign suppliers and trading partners had a website or online presence in related industry directories, creating an online presence through a website and other online directories became a pertinent objective for the company. Additionally, Alomo Bitters, the firm's major product, had been named the 1999 product of the year by CIMG. The firm therefore considered marketing its brands and itself globally through the Internet. Consequently, the firm contracted its ISP to design a website for the firm. The website consisted of three main web pages: a) Home/About Us – description of company with its activities; b) Products – product description; and c) Contact

Us – company's contact details. The expected value was the firm's perceived benefits of an online presence and visibility. The website was hosted by the ISP, as a sub-domain under the ISP's domain – http://www.aoghana.com.gh/kasadrin. An email address was created for the firm based on the ISP's domain. The website was allocated 10mb server space and email address – kasadrin@aoghana.com.gh. Its usage statistics were not monitored and no updates were done on the website in 2001.

In summary, we identify three key actions used by the firm to acquire resources and use them to develop an informational e-commerce capability which further supported or partly enabled the achievement of informational and operational benefits. The actions are:

- Learning from trading partners;
- Using external IS resources to address internal IS resource poverty; and
- Using Internet and email to support core activities such as sourcing and maintaining business relationships with production material suppliers.

The informational and operational benefits partly enabled by the capability are creating an online presence and marketing the firm's products; and initiating and supporting transactions and business relationships with production material suppliers.

Interactional E-commerce Capability (Jan 2002 – Jul 2007)

The development of an interactional e-commerce capability in KCL is characterised by two interrelated stages: development of an IS infrastructure which facilitated the implementation of an IT strategy which included developing an interactive website. First, KCL sought to automate its internal operations and business processes. The firm purchased a bundle of software – accounting, payroll, and a fleet management system from a local IT software development firm, PERF. PERF was responsible for upgrading KCL's existing IT infrastructure – buying computers and networking them to support the running of the software. When the project was completed the firm realised they needed an IT support staff or team to manage the IS infrastructure. KCL asked the project manager to develop an IT strategy for the firm and later recruited the project manager as their IS manager. Another IT technician was also recruited to work in unison with the IS manager. These human and technical resources became a precursory foundation to enable the firm to enhance its IT capabilities and develop other e-commerce capabilities including the design of an interactive website.

On appointment, the IS manager (hereafter referred to as Sarah) began to implement the IT strategy which included subscription to a broadband Internet service (2003), the development of an interactive website (2003), and initiation of an enterprise resource planning system to integrate all data and functional processes in the firm (2006-2008). In developing the website, Sarah researched websites of beverage companies (worldwide) in order to get ideas to inform the content. Sarah comments that,

> 'The old website was very basic and compared to the websites of other foreign beverage companies, it was less informative and had spelling mistakes. It was not a good representation of the company's growing reputation, locally and internationally'.

After the research, the design concepts were discussed with CT Solutions, whom the project was outsourced to. A proposal with a preliminary design developed through this collaboration was presented to the firm's management team for an evaluation. The website was considered as a critical part of the company's measures to respond to the growing competition in the industry. Decisions made on the website included the choice of colour, the graphics and the content; the choice of a Flash-based website for fast Internet connection and a non-Flash-based website for slow Internet connection; and the integration of the firm's local distributorship network into the website content (in the form of an online directory). In reference to the company's commitment to social responsibility, a caution on being of a legal drinking age before entering the site was incorporated in the website design. The new website was designed by June 2003. A new domain name was registered – www.kasadringh.com. It was hosted on a 1000MB server web space in the USA through CT Solutions. The company pays US$60 a month for the web hosting. The website consisted of six main web pages:

- Products Page – detailed description of all products;
- Company Page – provides information on the company mission, vision and board of directors;
- Distributors Page – a directory listing the contact details of distributors by region and offering downloadable application forms;
- News – latest news and events on the company's products and activities;
- Downloads – offers wallpapers on company products;
- Contact Us – offers an enquiry form to make enquiries and provides contact information and location direction to the firm.

Exhibit 8 shows the homepage of the www.kasadringh.com (flash version).

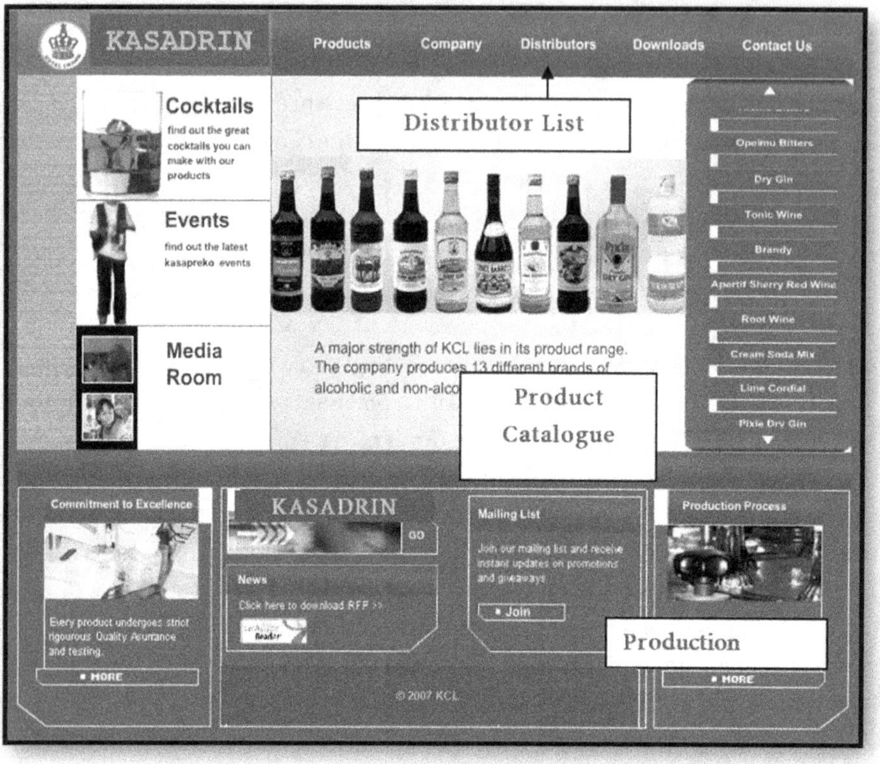

Exhibit 8 Homepage of the www.kasadringh.com (flash version)

Though there was no search functionality on the website, a product combo-box was placed on the homepage to facilitate easy navigation to any product. In addition to the main pages of the website, there are three other sub-pages; Media Room, Events and Cocktails. These pages were used to create a form of social connotation or interaction with the firm's potential customers/consumers of their products. Media room made available video adverts run through TV networks, and the cocktails page featured related cocktails which could be prepared with their products. Information on all offline events and promotions of products are also made available online on the Events Page. The firm also attempted to increase its visibility by providing a view of its production process and information on quality assurance procedures employed by the firm. However, this seems to have relatively had a minimal impact, since it is only a slideshow of three pictures depicting the production process. When questioned on using a better presentation medium, such as video, the Plant and Bottling manager explains that,

'We are, perhaps, the first or one of the first alcoholic beverage manufacturers in Ghana to develop a complete wall-to-wall automation of its production line, from bottling to packaging. Hence, for competitive reasons, the firm has reservations of making a public display of its machines in its production line. We therefore considered a few pictures of certain sections of the production line were enough to show our production line'.

Porter (1985: 33-34) states that: '...A firm gains competitive advantage by performing these strategically important activities more cheaply or better than its competitors'. Hence, in view of other competing products, the seeming objective was to protect knowledge on core resources and other key organisational information which help create this advantage from competitors. Thus, combining the automated production line with other organisational resources like research and development of new products (as done with Opeimu Bitters in 2005), and marketing (as done with the indigenous naming system for products) and managerial skills and knowledge, the firm can create a capability, such as market responsiveness (in product line), which may be rare across the competitors in the market (Santhanam and Hartono, 2003).

This reservation or relative sensitivity to the kind (and detail) of information made available on the Internet was also extended to information on KCL's financial performance, production volume and sales information. Notwithstanding, the OM argues that,

The reservations placed on publishing information on organisational performance and production capacity was relevant in designing the website as of 2003, however much has changed since then. Other leading manufacturing firms in Ghana are making available their press releases of performance both in local press and on their websites. By providing this information, we have a better chance of enhancing the reputation and credibility we seek to create online and inform the decision-making process of prospective trading partners and customers'.

Incomplete or asymmetrical information could affect decision-making related to purchase which may lead to loss of contracts and contractual disputes (Pare, 2003). Hence, providing inadequate information affects the capability of using informational resources like the company's website to enhance the decision making of prospective customers and trading partners.

The challenge in using the website is to do with its management. The average number of page views per month was 148 in 2004; 227 (2005) and 348 (2006). Between 2003 and 2006, there have only been three major updates. The updates were done when a department – Human Resources, IT or Marketing – of the company needed to post new content on the website such as events and news. When questioned on the management of the website, Sarah comments that,

'I face a difficult situation of trying to convince the management on allocating more human resources for IT. I have requested for additional staff the past three years and this has not been met. From my observation, management responds to IT initiatives if only it is a recommendation by an external IT expert or consultant. For example, a request to buy and use corporate licensed copies of Microsoft products instead of single licensed or pirated copies installed by hired IT technicians were ignored until the Microsoft official representative in Ghana sent in a letter concerning a software inspection exercise. Hence, I have had to use consultants to initiate IT projects, such as upgrading software and purchasing new infrastructure.

Concerning the website, CT Solutions does not have enough interaction with us, as a client. After the website was designed, there was no further relationship and we were not advised on the management of the website. CT Solutions only contacts us when there is a need to renew the web hosting contract or any other form of service which requires payment. Moreover, we receive about 10 emails each week on new enquiries concerning our products and business activities, but since there is no specific employee to respond and follow-up on these enquiries, we just forward them to the head of department of relevance. This often leads to information overload and some of the enquiries are therefore not attended to. The IT unit does not have resources to monitor the state of the enquiry and similar or related enquiries are made over time repetitively. If analysed the website could have been updated with the relevant information to relatively reduce the enquiries or make enquiries more relevant. As a result, we (the IT unit), do what we can with the limited resources'.

Previous literature has noted that scarcity of skilled personnel or the requisite IS human resources tends to be a limiting factor to the development and management of e-business within firms in developing countries (Singh and Gilchrist, 2002). To address the internal resource poverty, these firms use IT consultancies to create this online presence. However, IT consultancies, who are usually responsible for designing and hosting the websites, fail to give these firms any reports on website traffic and strategic advice on Internet marketing after the websites are developed. This could affect the achievement of expected value and the continuity of projects. The manager of CT Solutions argues that,

> 'There was no specific contract concerning the management of the website, hence there was no agreed deliverables. The firm paid US$60 monthly for the web hosting. The fact is that firms have poor understanding of the Internet. Most companies seek projects that deliver immediate results. Websites in this part of the world are not transactional, they are mostly used for branding, image promotion and information provision. We don't have the supporting systems for transactional websites. Hence, the firms do not put much value on websites since the results are not apparently immediate. Additionally, most organisations do not have a coherent web strategy that we can inform.
>
> What we, website developer firms, do, is to translate the website strategy of the firm into reality. With our experience, we can relatively suggest or recommend to companies about what they can do. Therefore, we provide some level of consultancy, but since the Internet is not tangible and we do not have privy access to all business information and processes, it is difficult to quantify returns to the firm. Moreover, most Ghanaian firms do not consider the Internet as their core business. Hence, because of this lack of intimacy, the switching costs are low and many firms do change their IT solution partners as soon as they fail to deliver or get disappointed about their services. That is the major challenge the firms face, the market (IT sector) is different here in Ghana'.

We note from the above that the social reputation, credibility and image of KCL tend to influence the choice of e-commerce technologies and allocation of resources to facilitate adoption and use. Thus, perhaps, without an apparent threat to these social resources, resource allocation for an e-commerce project may be stalled or considered less necessary. Faced with such constraints, the negotiation skills of KCL's IS manager became necessary to ensure the continuity of projects. For example, in January 2007, this impasse between KCL and CT Solutions was resolved after a management meeting was arranged internally between the IT Unit and management team and externally between the KCL and CT Solutions. The IS manager argued on the necessity to update the website in time for Ghana's Independence anniversary (in which KCL was a key sponsor). The OM also emphasised the need to advertise the new fluorescent bottle cap for Opeimu Bitters, which had been changed in response to the piracy of the product. As part of this update, the flash website was dropped, and a non-flash website was updated with new pictures and navigation buttons to every part of the website. The flash website was dropped because, as compared to the non-flash website, it required more time and detail to be updated and the firm did not have the internal requisite skill and time availability to perform such updates. Dropping the flash website was therefore a response to the resource poverty in the firm. The firm was also provided with a simple administrative interface for updates and editing of content.

In summary, we identify five key actions used by the firm to acquire resources and use them to develop an interactional e-commerce capability which further enabled the achievement of largely strategic and informational benefits. The actions are:

1. Investing in requisite IT infrastructure;
2. Enhancing managerial business and IS knowledge and skills with new employees;
3. Prototyping website with knowledge from global benchmarks in the beverage industry;
4. Integrating the local distributorship network into website content; and
5. Joint evaluation of website (interactive) content by management and the IS consultant.

The informational and operational benefits partly enabled by the capability are creating an online presence and marketing the firm's products; and initiating and supporting transactions and business relationships with production material suppliers. Further, these benefits generated strategic benefits in terms of:

- Export of 5000 cartons of Alomo Bitters generated through an email request;

The other strategic benefits are:

- New product development and cost-savings from curbing product piracy through a partnership (email initiated and sustained) with an Indian bottle cap manufacturer; and

- Supporting firm policy of having two key suppliers for production materials through sourcing and maintaining relationships with production material suppliers.

Managing Resources to Address Constraints

This section identifies key business and e-commerce constraints and evaluates how KCL managed resources to address them and achieve benefits.

Addressing Competition

Piracy or imitation of KCL's products has been a major constraint to the firm's business. In 2002, the company began to receive complaints about imitated or fake products, specifically Alomo Bitters, on the Ghanaian market. From a market study, KCL realised that the only way they could prevent imitation of their products, was to develop product seals which could not be copied or locally produced in Ghana. This was to be in the form of security caps; thus changing their embossed bottle caps to chamfered bottle caps (caps which have beveled edges). KCL contacted its cap supplier in Italy and other related European companies to ascertain whether they could develop chamfered caps for their bottles. However, it failed to find a company that could produce such caps.

In 2003, KCL received an email from an Indian company, which expressed the interest of producing caps for them after visiting their website. It was during these email discussions that the Indian firm confirmed that they could produce chamfered caps for their products. The Indian firm began to produce chamfered caps for the firm in 2003 after sample products were approved and each firm's credibility was established through the bankers of both firms. The success in curbing the piracy of Alomo Bitters has also led to the development of new fluorescent green caps to curb the piracy of Opeimu Bitters in 2006.

Extant literature has emphasised a number of the regulatory constraints in Ghana. These include the ineffectiveness of legal institutions to enforce laws establishing rights and intellectual property (Mensah, 2004: 12), and the high cost of settling claims and excessive delays in court procedures (Arthur, 2006: 41). Though legislative reviews were considered as part of Ghana's e-commerce strategy, the above issues presuppose that these challenges are yet to be addressed. Thus firms like KCL have to find other means of addressing issues of piracy and copyright of products. This occurred through developing product parts (bottle caps) which could not be easily substituted or copied. The searching, selecting and negotiating with the Indian firm was greatly enabled by the firm's access to and use of the Internet and e-mail. This partnership also helped to address similar occurrences in the piracy of other products. We note that the constraints of the context partly, became a precursor for innovation within the firm; thus the firm draws on its resources to circumvent its constraints and achieve its objectives.

Managing Online Relationships

Production materials and equipment tend to be a bundle of key resources needed to support the production processes in KCL. KCL has a policy of keeping two suppliers for production materials to avoid or reduce delays in production in the event of unplanned circumstances. The searching, selecting/evaluation, and negotiating with foreign suppliers are greatly enabled by the firm's access to and use of the Internet, its website and e-mail. Quite often, the MD is also involved in searching for suppliers through the Internet. He usually initiates the search through Google and the result list is evaluated with the management team. Emails are sent by the MD to selected suppliers to initiate the business relationship and negotiate on purchase prices, after which the OM, PSM and the other managers work on the other contractual agreements and credibility checks to place the order. The firm's Web presence also facilitates online credibility in order to initiate these business relationships. The GFA claims that the use of the Internet to search and obtain supplier details and email for communication, has improved the efficiency of management, by reducing communication costs in terms of time and brought the firm closer to its suppliers of goods and services in Europe and India.

Despite the IS resource issues highlighted by Sarah, the GFA explains that,

'In terms of communication, email makes it easier especially because of the time differences with the suppliers in India and with the different levels of English proficiency and language accents which affect voice communication over telephone. Additionally, it also facilitates the contractual agreements and transactional processes – purchase requests, order confirmation, electronic copies of Letters of Credits (which are received from banks and forwarded to suppliers), and delivery notification.'

This argument draws attention to communication barriers that occur through verbal communication over telephone and the timeliness of information delivery. However, having access to the Internet and email may not be necessarily enough to engender trust and compliance which are essential to sustain these online business relationships. It is the compliance mechanisms and the firm's commitment to them which engenders trust (Pare, 2003). In this respect, first, KCL supports these online relationships with transparency and relative timeliness of fulfilling contractual agreements. For example, the first time the firm received credit of US$15,000 for the purchase of alcohol, KCL managed to pay within the due date, which led to other opportunities for credit from the supplier. As a result, the MD made it a firm policy to fulfill payments on orders given on credit, on time. This helped them to establish a financial credibility with their material suppliers and to attract further credit in other negotiations. Second, the firm uses business visits to enhance email-driven and -supported business relationships with international trading partners. For example, in terms of the Indian suppliers, both companies have had the opportunity of visiting each other's factory after the business relationship was established. The OM comments that,

'These visits help in enhancing business relationships and the image of the firm through the establishment of inter-personal relationships and familiarisation with the firm's activities'.

These findings tend to be congruent with Kuada's (2002) study on the strategic alliances between Danish and Ghanaian companies. The study pointed out that visiting the premises of firms enables both parties to make the honest assessment of resources and capabilities, especially before entering into partnerships. Yet, though email enables relatively timely communication of information with international trading partners, it tends to be different with local trading partners and institutions. The OM comments that,

'With most of the emails sent within Ghana, especially to government agencies, you have to let the person know beforehand that you would be sending an email to the person before you do so, otherwise you may not get a response on time or the person may even deny receipt of the mail'.

This tends to emphasize how existing or preferred patterns of communications influence the extent of adoption and usage of non-verbal communication innovations in the Ghanaian culture. More verbal communication tends to be one of the characteristics of cultures with rich interpersonal communication like Ghana (Bajaj and Leonard, 2004).

Impact of E-commerce Activities

The notable contribution of e-commerce at the firm-level has earlier been identified in the summary of e-commerce capabilities discussions. Concerning development, though the firm has created employment opportunities (101 permanent and 150-180 temporary) no claims can be made concerning the extent to which e-commerce directly or indirectly supported or created the opportunities. We can make note that though this may be relatively farfetched, e-commerce in supporting production processes and efforts to curb piracy, may have supported organisational performance which is a key enabler to supporting these employment opportunities.

Questions

1. What benefits are Ghanaian firms obtaining from e-commerce adoption?
2. What resources do Ghanaian firms use to develop e-commerce capabilities?
3. How do Ghanaian firms develop and deploy resources to create capabilities which achieve e-commerce benefits?

References

Arthur, P. (2006) The State, Private Sector Development, and Ghana's "Golden Age of Business", *African Studies Review*, 49(1), 31–50.

Bajaj, A. and Leonard, L.N.K. (2004) The CPT Framework: Understanding the Roles of Culture, Policy and Technology in Promoting E-Commerce Readiness, *Problems and Perspectives in Management*, 3, 242-252.

Ghana Club 100 (2004). *2002/3 Ghana Club 100 Report*, Volume 6, October, Accra, Ghana: Ghana Club 100.

Ghana Club 100 (2005). *2004 Ghana Club 100 Report*, Volume 7, October, Accra, Ghana: Ghana Club 100.

Mensah, S. (2004) 'A Review of SME Financing Schemes in Ghana', Paper Presented at the *UNIDO Regional Workshop of Financing Small and Medium Scale Enterprises*, Accra,

Pare, D.J. (2003). Does This Site Deliver? B2B E-Commerce Services for Developing Countries, *Information Society*, 19(2), 123-134.

Porter, M.E. (1985). *Competitive Advantage: Creating and Sustaining Superior Performance*, New York, NY: Free Press.

Santhanam, R. and Hartono, E. (2003). Issues in Linking Information Technology Capability to Firm Performance, *MIS Quarterly*, 27(1), 125-153.

Factors which Influence Mobile Banking Adoption

Nana Yaa Sika Ofori, Desmond Ateh Larkai and Naa Odoley Yehowadah Oddoye

> The primary purpose of this case study is to identify important deployment factors for mobile banking technology in the banking sector. The data was collected from ABC Bank and it was selected because of its extensive provision of various mobile banking services.

Profile of ABC Bank Ghana Limited

ABC Bank Ghana Limited is one of the largest banks in terms of assets and a tier 1 bank in the country. It was established in Ghana in 1999 and now has 36 branches and 78 ATMs which are located across the country. Responsible corporate citizenship is very much valued at ABC Bank Ghana. This is reflected in the bank's business principles and practices, and its community support policies and programmes. By focusing on education, health and entrepreneurship among others, the bank ensures that it remains environmentally, culturally and socially relevant. Accolades received by the ABC Bank Ghana include; Best Bank in Sub Custodian Service 2015, and Best Commercial Bank 2014, and Best Investment Bank in Ghana 2015.

Theoretical Lens: Technology Organization Environment (TOE) Model

Tornatzky and Fleischer (1990) developed the Technology-Organization-Environment (TOE) framework that describes how technological innovation adoption occurs at firm level. The TOE framework suggests that there are three elements namely; **Technological Context, Organizational Context** and **Environmental Context** that have an impact on a firm's adoption process of technological innovation.

The first element of the TOE framework which is the Technological Context, refers to the relevant internal and external technology available to the firm. Technology itself is merely a physical tool, but it involves knowledge, where a person has to interact with the technology to know the purpose of using it, how to operate the tool, and the impact of using it.

The Organizational Context refers to the organizational characteristics such as firm size, the structure and the complexity of the managerial structure of top management. Apart from the formal linking structures of management, the organizational context covers the informal decision making and communication processes between employees. Besides, the firm's human resource quality, the availability of slack resources (financial and human resources) also reflect the Organizational Context.

Lastly, in the Environmental Context, TOE framework embraces the fact that, to adopt a new technology, an organization has to interact with its surrounding business environment. The business environment refers to entities that exist in their industry which include customers, suppliers, competitors in the industry, obligations from government regulatory bodies and other external pressures. These entities may act as constraints and/or opportunities for an organization's technological adoption.

Using the TOE framework, the next section examines the adoption of mobile banking technology in ABC Bank.

Technology

Complexity
Perceived complexity is the degree to which an innovation or technology is perceived as difficult to understand and use. The case findings indicate that about 10% of the bank's customers have subscribed to their new mobile technology. There has not been any official complaint about the sophistication of the technology, as the technology was made very easy to use and understand. As the Head of operations stated clearly:

We hold our customers in high esteem and so we did not want to deploy any technology that would be very difficult to use. The complexity of the technology was taken into consideration before deploying it.

The non- complexity of the technology which was taken into consideration during the deployment process makes the customers enthusiastic about the adoption and use of the mobile banking technology.

Relative advantage

Perceived superiority and relative advantage are among the significant factors that influenced the deployment of the mobile banking technology at ABC Bank. The advantages include improved customer service, business efficiency, and cost reduction. With regard to customer service, ABC Bank was able to reduce counter pressure and waiting time through the direction of certain functions to the mobile applications. Additionally, the mobile banking provides convenience, ease of access and use. Furthermore, the technology has promoted more efficient and effective business processes in the activities of ABC Bank, by addressing the fast increasing retail banking transaction volumes without additional staffing costs. This is indicated in the interview with the Digital Support Officer,

The deployment of mobile banking has translated into the reduction of counter pressure because customers no longer come into the banking halls. They only come to the banking hall if it is really necessary....

Organization

Top Management

McAlearney (2006) summarizes that great leadership must be transformational and leaders must be able to empower and motivate their employees, define and articulate a vision, build and foster trust and relationships, as well as adhere to accepted values and standards. They must be able to inspire their employees to accept change, meet organizational objectives on multiple levels, and build a strong brand name for their business. However, it is very important to consider whether leadership development in ABC Bank had a strong impact on the deployment of organizational innovation capabilities, like its mobile banking technology. As one employee of the bank stated:

> ...in this world, we are moving towards IT so if you are not IT inclined, you will be left out. So as a bank, if you don't do these things, you fall out especially now that technology keeps changing. In other words, the top management is aware of these innovations and does not need anybody to prompt them on it before implementing the technology. It's natural, everybody agreed to it, especially having in mind the satisfaction of customers.

Therefore, we conclude that top management support positively impacts on mobile banking deployment in ABC Bank.

Environment

Competitive Pressure

ABC bank was not pressured by competition to adopt mobile banking technology. ABC bank Ghana is already aware it is operating in a competitive environment and therefore needs to be more proactive in mobile banking technology in order to attract and retain its customers. For instance, when ABC bank made its debut into the banking industry in Ghana in 2000, the industry was dominated by many local and a few international banks. Bank of Ghana was then the largest market share holder offering all kinds of services to the public sector workers; the majority of the country's workforce. In order to survive, the bank's challenge was to provide quality services rapidly at affordable prices by making the right connections to create and enhance value for customers, and other stakeholders. As the Digital Support Officer said:

> It is competitive to deploy mobile banking. Even though some banks had deployed the technology before us, our main reason for deploying the mobile banking technology was to expand our territories to reach many customers at different places. We already know what to do to maintain our customers. We did not deploy the technology because others had done same.

It was not only the case that other banks in the industry were deploying the mobile banking technology and that led ABC Bank Ghana to deploy, but rather because ABC Bank intention was to deploy a superior technology.

Customer Expectations

Since customer expectations serve as a standard or reference point against which performance is measured or judged, ABC Bank Ghana provided their customers with mobile accounting services, mobile brokerages services and financial information services, bearing customer expectations like reliability, speed, and convenience in mind.

It was found that consumers' demand for a greater variety of mobile banking services was a factor that influenced the bank to deploy the mobile banking technology in Ghana. The fear of losing customers to other banks was also a major factor that influenced ABC Bank to deploy the technology. However, the value systems, behaviour and attitude of Ghanaian people have gradually changed from trust worthy and peaceful to a culture characterized by distrust and uncertainty. This culture makes the endorsement of mobile banking very difficult for banks. As a result of the distrust, ABC Bank has not successfully attracted new customers notwithstanding the marketing efforts to convince customers of the reliability and the credibility of the mobile services.

A Branch Manager explains that Ghanaian customers are curious and sceptical about the ability of the legal system of Ghana to protect their interests and to assure their security and convenience (concerning electronic transactions). Because of this, a lot more people are reluctant to subscribe to the services although they are free. He said:

There are a few people on it but compared to the account retail base, subscription is very low. Roughly it's only about 10% of customers that are currently using it.

He added:

Our main issue is our customers' perception about legislations. Though we constantly convince them that legislations are already in place, they seem pessimistic as though they have not heard about these. Even so, they do not trust the legislations because the legislations may not be mature. (Branch Manager).

Indeed, customer expectation is one of the most important factors ABC bank took into consideration before deploying the technology. However, due to the behaviour and attitude of most customers characterized by distrust, the use of mobiles for banking made the customer subscription as low as 10% in the year 2014. The value systems, behaviour and attitude of Ghanaian people have made the endorsement of mobile banking very difficult for banks. As a result of the distrust, ABC Bank has not been able to attract new customers notwithstanding the marketing efforts to convince customers of the reliability and the credibility of the mobile banking services.

Research Questions

1. What factors affect the adoption of mobile banking in banks in Ghana?
2. What strategic steps can banks use to aid the adoption of mobile banking in Ghana?

Enhancing Livelihoods through Mobile Business

Richard Boateng and Sheena Lovia Boateng

> This case study explores how a micro-entrepreneur develops and sustains his livelihood through a mobile business enterprise.

Background Information

Abubakari Sulley (A.S) is a single 22 year old Technical student who is currently studying automobiles at a private vocational institution in Kaneshie, Accra. He enrolled in his current institution for practical experience in automobiles after completing SHS where he did only the theoretical aspect. Currently he lives at Dansoman Last Stop. He pays his own rent, utility and living expenses. His monthly rent is GHc 25; electricity expense is GHc 5 monthly. He does not pay water bills. There is no water supply in his home so he rather buys water. His living expenses in a month amount to Ghc 250. He has no dependants.

Current Business Information and Start-up Story

Exhibit 9 Mobile Kiosk of Abubakari Sulley

A.S has been involved in M-business for 4 years. He acquired a kiosk to use for his M-business activities from his friend at the cost of Ghc 350.00 in his second year of business. He changed his location when the kiosk he currently uses was put up for sale (Exhibit 9). The kiosk was sold along with 3 phones and 2 transfer SIM cards. Presently, the location of his business can be classified as both residential and market. This is because his location is adjacent Dansoman Military Barracks but directly opposite Dansoman Fire Station, which is situated inside Dansoman Community Market. His current mobile business activities are: the sale of airtime vouchers, credit transfers, voice call popularly known as 'space to space', SIM card sales and registration for five out of the six network operators in Ghana namely: Airtel, MTN, Vodafone, TiGo and Glo. He also does mobile cash transfer for MTN known as Mobile Money. When asked whether he is involved in any other business apart from the M-business, he responded,

'No, it's the sole business with which he gets his daily bread'.

A.S mentioned one Ben as his supplier. Initially, he used to buy from a wholesale shop nearby and still does sometimes. When asked how he got to know Ben his supplier, he mentioned Ben passed by one day and introduced himself as supplier of all network airtime vouchers and credit transfer. He said there was no registration involved and the terms and conditions was solely cash and carry; but as they got to know themselves better he could supply him with airtime in advance and he would pay later. A.S gets supplies from the wholesale shop when Ben can't make it or would be late the next day to supply A.S who may run out of stock.

When asked about what he did previously, he mentioned that he had nothing doing in the house after completing junior high school so he helped a friend who was involved in the same business at Dansoman Sahara. His stepmother suggested he work for someone in the same business closer to her chop bar. However, he refused and decided to start his own M-business thinking his stepmother just wanted a way for him to help with her chopbar (local restaurant) operations. He started his business at Dansoman Children's Park opposite New Century School before he moved to his current location at Dansoman market. He began with the sale of airtime vouchers and voice calls (space to space). On starting he had the sum of Ghc 30 at hand from his personal savings which he used to buy the airtime vouchers, an old table from the friend he helped and his personal phone which he used for the voice calls. After the first month he bought a credit transfer chip at a cost of Ghc 30 which he used to transfer credit to customers. Since he had no extra phone for the credit transfer he would take out his personal SIM and put the transfer chip in his phone anytime he had a customer who requested for the credit transfer.

It was a big challenge since that practice could weaken the phone. After the second month in business, he acquired a slightly used handset at a cost of Ghc 15 at circle with the money given to him by his dad. The first person he sold to was a bread seller. His first day and month sales were Ghc 3.30 and Ghc 38 respectively. He started with the sale of MTN, Vodafone, TiGo and Airtel recharge vouchers and then added the transfer of credit after 2 months. In 2012, the need for SIM registration became mandatory so he engaged in that business as well. He added mobile cash transfer early this year.

A.S. has been able to open another branch at Dansoman Children's Park in July 2013. He acquired the kiosk for the new branch at the cost of Ghc200.00.

Operational Issues

Looking at the financial earnings, he pointed out that the credit transfer is the bestselling M-business activity; with MTN and TiGo being the bestselling network voucher, TiGo and Airtel being the bestselling SIM cards with Expresso being the poorest selling network voucher. He also chose MTN as the most patronized credit transfer network. Since the only mobile cash transfer he is involved in is MTN mobile money he couldn't tell which of the networks mobile cash transfer is most patronized but he was of the view that mobile money was highly patronized and hence 'lucrative'.

When asked how much he earned on each M-business activity he said he earned:

at least Ghc 0.04 for each Ghc1 airtime voucher, Ghc 0.08 for each Ghc 2 airtime voucher, Ghc 0.25 for each Ghc 5 airtime, Ghc 0.40 for each Ghc 10 airtime voucher sold for all networks, Ghc 0.20 for each minute on voice calls, Ghc 4 for each Ghc 30 mobile cash transfer, Ghc 0.10 for every Ghc 1 credit transfer.

A.S. has seven special customers who buy from him alone, sometimes when they meet his absence at his location they contact him, go back to their house and return later. At other times too they only have to call if they need credit and he would send it to them. They also buy in higher denominations. A.S' family members buy from him too. Currently, he owns four phones. Three for the M-business and one personal phone: a Samsung E1205T for MTN credit transfer and SIM registration, a Samsung GT 1085F for Airtel calls and registration, a Nokia 5030C for TiGo transfer and SIM registration and a Sony Ericsson as his personal phone.

AS' average daily profit from his M-business activities is estimated as Ghc 13.00, his average daily savings is Ghc 10 and monthly profit is Ghc300.

Benefits

When asked how much training he has received in operating the M-business, he indicated that for SIM registration and the mobile cash transfer, formal training was given by the respective mobile network operators but for the credit transfer he followed the instructions provided on the kit when he obtained the SIM. He also added that any time he faced a challenge in operating any of his business activity he sought help from the service providers and they responded accordingly.

In response to the extent to which he agrees the business is financially rewarding he strongly agreed saying

'It is even out of this business that I pay my school fees, admission fees, utilities and other living expenses'.

When asked the extent to which the business has enabled him acquire any of the livelihood assets, he said for human capital, he strongly agreed that it has offered him employment and also to acquire new skills and personal development. He added that he has been equipped on how to relate to people and manage customers as well as how to carry himself well. He again agreed that for financial capital, though he has not tried it he believes it is possible to get access to credit because of the business and when asked whether it has helped him start saving in any formal financial institution he responded "no" but added that he keeps the money himself due to an experience he had with one of the formal banks. He is of the view that, though he hasn't bought a land yet, he could do so anytime he is ready. When asked whether the business has helped reinforce relationships, he answered positively and for building social business networks he agreed using his supplier as an example; in that he could now supply him and he would pay later because of his ability to fulfil his financial needs. He added that there are times he would just call when he runs out of stock of credit transfer units and he would send him some. He further stated that the M-business has enabled him build new social business networks. He strongly agreed to the fact that he is able to pay and get access to utilities as well as the payment of tax and fees when the need arises, out of the business.

Vulnerability, Threats and Challenges

He feels secure because he is close to the barracks and also because the Ghana National Fire Service is just around him with the military and policemen patrolling day and night. He also pointed out that a change in the weather doesn't have much effect on the business. For instance, when it rains he doesn't stop work but closes the windows of the kiosk and stays in till it stops. He mentioned network interference to have little adverse effect on the business, because he has been provided with a different method for recharging airtime for customers when there is a network failure by the service providers.

He stated that competition doesn't affect his business because he has his own customers who don't buy from anybody apart from him unless he is not around. He also added that he has established a very good relationship with most of those who buy from him to the extent that he could send them airtime on their demand with just a phone call and payments are made later.

He indicated that family obligations sometimes affect the business; in that where there are some financial contributions to make and he does not have enough personal savings, he has to borrow from the business thereby reducing the amount of stock he would purchase the next time.

For financial capital limitations, it greatly affects the business because more profits are earned when vouchers are bought in large quantities and in large denominations so where you have limited finance you are unable to buy more and in large denominations which sell fast. Thus, it is likely to lose customers who would want none other than higher denominations, though some may not care.

He mentioned voucher accessibility to have a negative effect on the business because where he runs out of stock and the wholesale is far from his location, he is likely to lose some of the sales for the day since some customers may be unwilling to wait till his return. Beyond these, there are unforeseen conflicts which arise. He noted that

> 'There are times conflicts arise between the customers and me, where after recharging for them, some or all the credit is deducted for reimbursement of mobile credit loans taken by customers for which they have forgotten about and hence, they now think I didn't recharge for them. In such cases, I have to be patient and explain that their debts have taken up the value of their recharge'.

He pointed out that educational level has an effect on the types of M-business you can engage in. Unlike the sale of airtime vouchers which doesn't require literacy, SIM registration, Credit transfer, Mobile cash transfer and others require some formal education and training. One without basic education may not be able to operate these services.

Acknowledgements

Authors appreciate the support of Stella Quayson and Elizabeth Abakah during the data collection.

Questions

1. What are the factors that determine selection into mobile business entrepreneurship?
2. What facilitates/constraints mobile business operations?
3. What are the outcomes/benefits experienced by micro-enterprises in mobile business and how do these outcomes influence or impact their livelihood?

Using Theories to analyze Case Studies

Defining Theory

The definition of theory can be taken from different perspectives, depending on the objective of the definition. In terms of its consistent elements or components, a theory can be conceptualized as

> "a system of constructs and propositions that conjointly demonstrates a logical and yet systematic and coherent account of a phenomenon bounded by some assumptions and conditions" (Bacharach, 1989).

On the other hand, in terms of its purpose, a theory can also be viewed as a

> "coherent set of general propositions used as principles of explanation, understanding and/or prediction of the apparent relationships of certain observed phenomena" (Zikmund, 2003). A theory has been empirically tested and verified and can be shown as a schematic diagram, mathematical equation and words.

In its essence, a theory presents a way of studying concepts or variables concerning a phenomenon in order to find or investigate the solution for a research problem. A theory also explains or predicts occurrences by outlining the relationships between concepts or variables which underpin a phenomenon. However, to offer explanations or predictions, theories tend to possess certain characteristics. These characteristics, espoused by academics (Gregor, 2006; Bhattacherjee, 2012), include:

- Theory is not data, facts, typologies, taxonomies or empirical findings. Theories are not an ad hoc collection of constructs without relationships; they must have propositions (relationships), explanations, and boundary conditions.
- The explanations offered by theories are nomothetic. Thus, they tend to go beyond explaining single events to offer explanations which are generalizable across situations, events, or people. As such, they are less precise, less complete and tend to focus on patterns of events, behavior or phenomena.
- Theories operate at a conceptual level and stem from logic; however, data and findings operate at the empirical or observational level.

For a theory to be well understood, there are some foundational premises that need to be set. These are constructs, propositions, logic, and boundary conditions or assumptions (Bhattacherjee, 2012). The constructs of a theory define what the theory is about and also explain what concepts are important for understanding a phenomenon. Propositions, on the other hand, are about how these concepts are related to each other. The logic of a theory explains why the concepts are related and the boundary conditions or assumptions probe the "who, when, and where" by bringing out the circumstances under which these concepts and relationships work.

For the purposes of the case studies in this book, two theories are presented in this section. These theories have received much attention in strategic management and business studies, and are relevant in examining the Choices, Chances and Changes experienced by the firms and institutions in the case studies.

Resource-Based Theory (RBT) and Dynamic Capabilities (DC) Framework

Defining Resources: Assets and Capabilities

RBT tends to be the prevailing paradigm that explains or helps to understand how and why firms develop the capability to gain and sustain competitive advantage (Penrose, 1995; Wernerfelt, 1984; Barney, 1991). Its later extension, the dynamic capabilities approach examines how these firms adapt and even capitalize on rapidly changing technological or volatile environments as in DCs (Teece *et al.*, 1997). Within these theoretical frameworks, rival firms are viewed to compete on the basis of their internal characteristics, resources, through which they build competitive advantage and a superior long-term performance (Wernerfelt, 1984; Barney, 1991; Wade & Hulland, 2004).

Traditional strategic analysis considers a firm's resources as strengths that a firm uses *to conceive of and implement their strategies* (Learned et al., 1969; Porter, 1981). These strengths include 'all assets, capabilities, organizational processes, firm attributes, information, knowledge, et cetera controlled by a firm that enable the firm to conceive and implement strategies which improve its efficiency and effectiveness' (Daft, 1983 cited in Barney, 1991: 101). This seemingly broader perspective of firm resources has been recently narrowed as 'assets and capabilities that are available and useful in detecting and responding to market opportunities' (Sanchez et al., 1996 and Christensen & Overdorf, 2000 cited in Wade & Hulland, 2004: 109). Assets are considered as anything tangible or intangible which a firm uses in 'its processes for creating, producing, and/or offering its products (goods or services) to a market, whereas capabilities are repeatable patterns of actions in the use of assets to create, produce, and/or offer products to a market' (Sanchez et al., 1996 cited in Wade & Hulland, 2004: 109). Other authors who tend to differentiate resources from capabilities; define resources as tangible or intangible assets or inputs to production, and capabilities as a *coordinated set of tasks* which utilize these assets for the purpose of achieving a particular end result. Both conceptualizations, however, agree that capabilities utilize assets to achieve a defined organizational objective.

Assets can be classified as tangible, intangible and personnel-based resources (Grant, 1991). Tangible assets include 'the financial capital and the physical assets of the firm such as plant, equipment, and stocks of raw materials'; intangible assets comprise 'assets such as reputation, brand image and product quality'; and personnel-based (or organizational) assets include technical know-how, managerial commitment, knowledge and skills, organizational culture, employee training and loyalty (Bharadwaj, 2000: 171). Assets are assembled, integrated and deployed within business processes to form the capabilities which an organization uses to improve its efficiency and effectiveness (Grant, 1991).

In a broader conceptualization, an organizational capability is 'a high-level routine (or collection of routines) that together with its implementing input flows, confer upon the organization's management a set of decision options for producing significant outputs of particular type' (Winter, 2000 cited in Winter, 2003: 991). This collection of routines can also be considered as being operational or dynamic depending on their ability to cause change (rates of change) or impact through their output in the organization. Operational or ordinary capabilities, also known as ordinary or 'zero-level' capabilities are 'those that permit a firm to 'make a living' in the short-term', while dynamic capabilities, are those that 'operate to extend, modify or create ordinary capabilities' (Winter, 2003: 991). Dynamic capabilities, from the dynamic capabilities approach (Teece et al., 1997) is 'an extension of the resource-based view of the firm that was introduced to explain how firms can develop their capability to adapt and even capitalize on rapidly changing technological environments' (Montealegre, 2002: 516). They are developed through the appropriate adaptation, integration, and reconfiguration of internal and external organizational assets, capabilities and business processes to respond to the dynamic business environment (Teece et al., 1997).

On the other hand, recent work by Wang & Ahmed (2007), in building on this conceptualization of capabilities, further explains that 'dynamic capabilities are the 'ultimate' organizational capabilities that are conducive to long-term performance, rather than simply a 'subset' of the capabilities, as Teece et al. (1997) suggest' (p. 36). The authors conceptualize capabilities in three classifications: capabilities (first order), core capabilities (second-order), and dynamic capabilities (third order). In their argument, firms deploy operational or ordinary capabilities to attain a desired goal which ensures their economic survival. Core capabilities are deployed when a bundle of resources are deployed in the strategic direction of the firm. Dynamic capabilities become the overarching capabilities which go beyond achieving economic survival and strategic objectives to ensure that a firm's performance is sustained in response to the threats and opportunities in its business environment. They enable a firm to develop core capabilities among other resources and deploy them to create and sustain a strategic advantage in its business environment. This makes them critical to a firm's performance in rapidly changing technological environments (Teece et al., 1997) and the volatile environments in DCs (Okoli & Mbarika, 2003). This transformation of resources occurs in a 'swift, precise and creative manner' in line with the threats and changes to its strategic orientation (Wang & Ahmed, 2007: 36).

A capability may therefore exist as an ordinary capability until it is deployed alongside other resources in the strategic orientation of the firm to become a core capability or address an environmental change and/or to sustain firm performance to become a dynamic capability. This also presupposes that the creative potential of these capabilities, or in broader perspective, resources, differs. One may then ask what makes these resources differ in their ability to enable a firm to create and sustain its performance in the marketplace. This leads us to consider the attributes of resources.

Resource Attributes

RBT posits that to create and sustain a competitive advantage or achieve a performance beyond that of its competitors in the marketplace, a firm's resources must be *heterogeneous* and *immobile*, and to have that potential, the resources must simultaneously have attributes of being valuable, rare, imperfectly imitable and not strategically substitutable or non-substitutable by other resources (Barney, 1991) – the VRIN conditions (Bowman & Ambrosini, 2003). The attributes are briefly explained as follows:

Valuable: For a firm's resource to be valuable, it must be able to help the organization conceive of and implement strategies capable of exploiting opportunities and neutralizing threats in its environment and thereby improve its efficiency and effectiveness (Barney, 1991). It must be able to generate rents - lower costs in delivering products than that of competitors or revenue from differentiating its products (goods or services) - to be captured by the firm (Bowman & Ambrosini, 2000). The resource remains appropriate for the rent generating activity when the costs of exploiting the resource do not offset the rents generated (Peteraf, 1993). For example, in the development of a new product in a manufacturing firm, the cost of exploiting a resource should not be more than the profits made from the new product; otherwise the value creation process becomes relatively unsustainable with time.

Rare: To create an organizational performance beyond economic survival, a resource has to be rare, uncommon or scarce in its distribution across the competitors in the market (Amit & Schoemaker, 1993). It should be rare in its functionality and not just its type – functionality lies in capabilities generated from a combination of resources such as tangible, intangible and organizational assets (Bharadwaj, 2000: 171). The lack of rare resources creates competitive parity, where no firm obtains a clear competitive advantage, but 'firms do increase their ability of economic survival' (Porter, 1980 cited in Barney, 1991: 107). Some types of resources like IT infrastructure are easily available on the market, however, when combined with other organizational resources like managerial skills and knowledge, organizations can create a functionality - market responsiveness or customer support capability - which may be rare across the competitors in the market (Santhanam & Hartono, 2003).

Imperfect Imitability: Resources become imperfectly imitable when it is more difficult for competing firms to replicate them (Bowman & Ambrosini, 2003: 291). These occur in the presence of isolating mechanisms (Rumelt, 1984); when, firstly, its occurrence or availability to the organization is due to its unique historical conditions; secondly, the link between resources and the firm's sustained competitive advantage is causally ambiguous, and lastly, resources themselves are socially complex in nature (Dierickx & Cool, 1989; Barney, 1991). These isolating mechanisms increase the costs of competing firms in imitating a successful firm's resources. When other competitors imitate a functionality or are able to obtain other resources capable of substituting that resource, the resource loses its ability to create a sustained competitive advantage or organizational performance, though it may be valuable to the organization and rare among rival firms. It thus becomes important for resources to be also imperfectly imitable, and beyond that, become not strategically substitutable by other resources.

Non-Substitutability: Substitutes can be in the form of imitating resources exactly or using different resources to create the effect of a resource as used in the successful firms. Competing firms are able to develop substitutes when they are able to discern the value-creation process and understand the value contributed by the resource possessed by the successful firm (Barney, 1991: 292). These substitutes are only valuable when competing firms are able to achieve a low-cost strategy for developing and exploiting the resource to achieve a value same as or superior to that of the successful firm. However, in the presence of the isolating mechanisms discussed earlier, discerning or understanding the value creation process of resources becomes difficult. This increases the costs of imitation and substitution, reducing the value or rents generated by the substitutes (Bowman & Ambrosini, 2003: 292).

In effect, RBT states that creating competitive advantage lies in the heterogeneity of valuable resources or in possessing resources that are valuable, appropriate and rare or uncommon across firms, and sustaining that advantage depends on them being imperfectly mobile; inimitable and non-substitutable (Barney, 1991; Wade & Hulland, 2004: 117-118). So then how does the concept of ordinary, core and dynamic capabilities fit in?

As earlier explained, dynamic capabilities go beyond ensuring the company's economic survival to enabling it to sustain and achieve new benefits thereby sustaining and improving its performance. Economic survival occurs when a company tends to have just valuable resources that enable it to obtain competitive parity. At this stage the resources may consist of largely ordinary capabilities, and perhaps a few core capabilities. However, the need to go beyond economic survival is arguably typical of the idiosyncratic institutional uncertainties in DCs (Okoli & Mbarika, 2003). Any change necessitating the detailed customization of the product, integration with other products, or extension of its functionalities to serve a specific or different target market requires the combination and reconfiguration of organizational assets and capabilities in order to achieve and sustain new benefits thereby sustaining and improving its performance (Winter, 2003: 991). In other scenarios such as the case of merger or acquisition at the firm-level or new developments in the national ICT infrastructure, a firm may expand its resource portfolio.

However, without deploying the new resources in, perhaps, the 'redefined' strategic direction of the firm, the rent generating ability of the new resources acquired may not be fully exploited. The firm may therefore need to develop higher order capabilities – core and dynamic – which extend the functionalities of existing and new assets and capabilities (largely ordinary), make them more rare, inimitable and not strategically substitutable and therefore increase their potential value contribution to a sustained organizational performance. Core capabilities are deployed when resources are oriented within the strategic orientation of the firm. Then in order to sustain the benefits achieved or respond to the threats (and/or opportunities) on core capabilities and performance of the firm, dynamic capabilities become necessary. These higher order capabilities therefore form part of a strategic process through which the firm develops, deploys and manages resources to sustain its performance in its rapidly changing or volatile business environment.

Dynamic Capabilities Framework

Though the resource-based theory is relevant in understanding resources, it is fairly quiet on how these resources are developed and deployed in firms. The notion that internal and external firm-specific resources, specifically capabilities, can be rebuilt or combined with other resources to develop new assets and capabilities lies in the dynamic capabilities framework, which until recent development by Teece at al. (1997) had been previously partially developed by Penrose (1959), Teece (1982) and Wernerfelt (1984).

The dynamic capabilities framework builds on theoretical foundations provided by Schumpeter (1934), Penrose (1959), Williamson (1975, 1985), Barney (1986), Nelson & Winter (1982) and Teece (1988) to give an understanding of how firms develop and renew their resources to be congruent to their rapidly changing environments (Dierickx & Cool, 1989; Prahalad & Hamel, 1990). Within this coherent framework, Teece *et al.* (1997: 518) argue that competitive advantage of a firm rests on its distinctive processes (managerial and organisational), and is shaped by its (specific) asset position, and the paths available to it by adoption or inheritance. The distinctive processes refer to the managerial and organisational processes by which things are done in the firm and in which the firm's capabilities are embedded; positions refer to the firm's current resource portfolio (owned and accessible); and paths refer to the strategic alternatives available to the firm. Capabilities and assets developed through paths should have the VRIN attributes to be considered as resources. Paths thus refer to the set of decision options through which capabilities and assets evolution occurs to create the significant outputs or the e-commerce benefits DC firms seek to achieve. This relates to our earlier conceptualisation of strategic orientation. Thus what a firm can do and where it can go tends to be constrained by its positions and paths (Teece et al., 1997: 524). This tends to be congruent with our earlier argument that a firm's ability to create and sustain e-commerce benefits depends on both its resources and strategic orientation.

The understanding of how resources, specifically capabilities, evolve through a set of possible paths is theoretically characterised by the capability lifecycle (Helfat & Peteraf, 2003: 1000). The capability lifecycle is defined by three main stages consisting of: the founding, developing and maturity stage; and then, after the maturity stage, the capability can branch into one of at least six additional stages of the lifecycle; retirement (death), retrenchment, renewal, replication, redeployment, and recombination, which influence the future evolution of the capability.

At the ***founding stage,*** the organisation identifies the objective of creating a new resource or specifically a new capability. The organisation would primarily have to rely on existing resources, or its current processes (embedded capabilities) and positions to create the new resources. The new resource may be created through the combination of existing resources to generate new ones or acquisition of new resources which also depends on the access created by present resources such as financial and social capital. What is thus required of the firm at this stage is to identify the necessary current assets positions and processes and organise them around the objective of developing a new resource. These may include forming a team to develop the capability for the firm (Helfat & Peteraf, 2003: 1000).

In the ***developing stage,*** the firm is required to develop the resource through a search and examination of viable alternatives for resource development. Teece *et al.* (1997) explain from the dynamic capabilities framework that through coordination, learning and reconfiguration organisational processes or embedded capabilities are developed. *Coordination* stems from recognising and examining the congruencies and complementarities among existing resources or current processes, and between them and assets positions. By identifying distinct ways of combining or coordinating resources, firms can create unique or firm-specific resources which may be imperfectly mobile and rare among competing firms. Then again, *learning* through repetition and experimentation enables the firm to acquire the tacit knowledge to perform its processes better and quicker, for existing processes to be innovated and for new processes to be identified (Levitt & March, 1988). Learning occurs at the individual and collective or organisational levels and internally in the organisation and externally from trading partners and competing firms (Dixon, 2000). For all learning opportunities, mechanisms should be created to make knowledge accessible for application in the improvement of existing resources and development of new resources in the organisation. Lastly, *reconfiguration*, involves the examination of the rapidly changing environment of the firm to transform or reconfigure a firm's assets structure and processes to sustain their strategic value to the firm. This capacity of reconfiguring and transforming itself is a learned organisational skill which is gained through practice (Teece *et al.*, 1997). After this stage when the resource becomes a learned organisational skill, its development may cease and enter the maturity stage.

The ***maturity stage*** is concerned with the maintenance of the resource; a capability which involves a lot of exercising or usage of the capability for it to become more habitual, and embedded in organisational memory and culture. As the resource becomes more tacit in nature, the development may fade away in the organisation and conditions of causal ambiguity and social complexity are created around the resource, making it imperfectly mobile (Barney, 1991; Helfat & Peteraf, 2003). After the maturity stage, the resource branches into at least one of the six additional stages of the lifecycle due to threats to the resource or capability. *Retirement* occurs when threats or extreme conditions force the firm to retire the resource entirely like prohibition of the sale of a specific product may retire the resource – such as manufacturing plants – that were used in producing and delivering that product (Helfat and Peteraf, 2003: 1006). Where the threats are less severe and do not suddenly retire the resource, it may initiate a gradual reduced utilisation of the resource like falling demand for product, and thus lead to *retrenchment*. On the other hand, certain threats or crises can rather give the firm the motivation to seek to improve a resource through renewal, redeployment and recombination, instead of retiring it. Alternatively, the organisation might even seek to enter a new product or geographic market which may redevelop the retired or retrenched resource. *Renewal* of resource requires the firm to enter a new development stage and search, examine and develop new alternatives. Renewal may lead to modification of resource as new alternatives may define changes in processes and assets positions. *Redeployment* occurs when the resource is redeployed into a market for a different but closely related product. Such transfers would require an alteration of the resource to enable it serve a different product market. The resource would thus have to enter a new development stage for it to be redeployed.

The firm may also reproduce the same resource in a different geographic market, thus *replicating* the resource. Since barriers to replication exist, the firm may experience an initial drop in the level of the resource (capability), and then redevelop it back to its pre-replication level. *Recombination* occurs when original resources are combined with other resources to form new resources. This can occur during the renewal of resources in a current product market or in transferring the resource to a different but related market. Ideally, renewal, redeployment and recombination may lead to substantial alteration of the original resource and on further development create a new resource *relatively* distinct from the old one (Helfat & Peteraf, 2003: 1008).

In effect, the capability lifecycle lends the understanding to the paths through which resources are developed, deployed and managed to create and sustain significant outputs or e-commerce benefits. The ability of the firm to carry out these resource development processes depends on the higher order – core and dynamic – capabilities in the firm. Coordination and learning to develop resources may occur through the deployment of core capabilities, however, the reconfiguration of resources in response to changes in a firm's business environment and to sustain e-commerce benefits would occur through the deployment of dynamic capabilities.

Sample Studies Using RBT and DC

1. Boateng, R. (2016). Resources, Electronic-Commerce Capabilities and Electronic-Commerce Benefits: Conceptualizing the Links, *Information Technology for Development, 22(6)*, 1-23.
2. Budu, J., and Boateng, R. (2015). Mobile Service Capabilities: evidence from a Ghanaian Mobile Service Provider. *International Journal of E-Services and Mobile Applications, 7(3)*, 1-17.
3. Chakrabarty, S., & Wang, L. (2012). The long-term sustenance of sustainability practices in MNCs: A dynamic capabilities perspective of the role of R&D and internationalization. *Journal of business ethics, 110* (2), 205-217.

4. Chirico, F., & Nordqvist, M. (2010). Dynamic capabilities and trans-generational value creation in family firms: The role of organizational culture. *International Small Business Journal, 28*(5), 487-504.
5. Cui, L., Zhang, C., Zhang, C., & Huang, L. (2006). Exploring e-government impact on Shanghai firms' Informatisation Process, *Electronic Markets, 16*(4), 312-328.
6. Montealegre, R. (2002). A process model of capability development: Lessons from the electronic commerce strategy at Bolsa De Valores De Guayaquil. *Organization Science, 13*(5), 514-531.
7. Zhu, K. and Kraemer, K.L. (2005). Post-adoption variations in usage and value of e-business by organizations: Cross country evidence from the retail industry. *Information Systems Research, 16*(1), 61-84.

Research Gaps in RBT

To guide future RBT and Information Systems (IS) research, extant research have emphasised two gaps of concern to this research. First, whether IS resources (like IS infrastructure and technical skills which have gained much focus in IS literature), must interact with other constructs – non-IS resources (like firm reputation and brand) – to create e-commerce benefits (Wade & Hulland, 2004: 124). The emerging success stories noted above are also suggestive of other non-IS resources such as social-cultural capital and networks being key resources to e-commerce adoption. Hence, research exploring how such non-IS resources interact with IS resources to create e-commerce benefits will be a welcome contribution to knowledge. Second, there are blurred distinctions between resources that help firms *attain* and those that help firms *sustain* competitive advantage (or performance). Further empirical research is considered as being critical to provide an understanding of "how firms get to be good, how they sometimes stay that way, why and how they improve and why they sometimes decline" (Teece *et al.*, 1997: 530).

Research Gaps in DC

The theory has been criticized for a number of issues. First, it does not define properly the term 'dynamic capabilities' (Arend & Bromiley, 2009). Others such as Eisenhardt and Martin (2000) indicate that 'dynamic capabilities' has been used vaguely in the literature. Second, in explaining dynamic capabilities in the literature, the firm is portrayed as a good performing one. Some have argued that poor-performing firms can also have dynamic capabilities (Rindova & Kotha, 2001) but that do not lead to success. Also, change has been misconstrued as success, but in actual fact, just because a firm does not change, does not indicate that it lacks the dynamic capabilities to change (Arend & Bromiley, 2009). Third, the theory has also received considerable criticism for its problems with measuring dynamic capabilities (Williamson, 1999). Pavlou and El Sawy (2011) have emphatically noted that there is a lack of a measurement model for the theory.

Key Readings on RBT and DC

1. Barney, J. (1991). Firm resources and sustained competitive advantage. *Journal of Management, 17*(1), 99-120.
2. Teece, D. J., Pisano, G. and Shuen, A. (1997). Dynamic capabilities and strategic management. *Strategic Management Journal, 18*(7), 509-533.
3. Wade, M. & Hulland, J. (2004). Review: The resource-based view and information systems research: Review, extension and suggestions for future research. *MIS Quarterly, 28*(1), 107-142.
4. Wang, C.L. & Ahmed, P.K. (2007). Dynamic capabilities: a review and research agenda, *International Journal of Management Reviews, 9*(1), 31-51.

References

Amit, R. and Schoemaker, P. (1993). Strategic Assets and Organizational Rent, *Strategic Management Journal, 14*(1), 33-46.

Arend, R., & Bromiley, P. (2009). Assessing the dynamic capabilities view: spare change, everyone? *Strategic Organization, 7*(1), 75.

Bacharach, S. B. (1989). Organizational Theories: Some Criteria for Evaluation, *Academy of Management Review, 14*(4) 496-515.

Barney, J. (1991). Firm resources and sustained competitive advantage. *Journal of Management, 17*(1), 99-120.

Barney, J. (1997). *Gaining and Sustaining Competitive Advantage*, Reading, MA: Addison-Wesley.

Barney, J. B. (1986). Types of Competition and the Theory of Strategy: Toward an Integrative Framework, *Academy of Management Review, 11*(4), 791-800.

Bharadwaj, A.S. (2000). A Resource-Based Perspective on Information Technology Capability and Firm Performance: An Empirical Investigation, *MIS Quarterly*, 24(1), 169-196.

Bhattacherjee, A. (2012). *Social Science Research: Principles, Methods, and Practices*, Florida: Global Text Project.

Bowman, C. and Ambrosini, V. (2000). Value Creation versus Value Capture: Towards a Coherent Definition of Value in Strategy, *British Journal of Management, 11*, 1-15.

Bowman, C. and Ambrosini, V. (2003). How the Resource-Based and The Dynamic Capability Views of the Firm Inform Corporate-level Strategy, *British Journal of Management, 14*, 289-303.

Christensen, C. M., and Overdorf, M. (2000). Meeting the Challenge of Disruptive Change, *Harvard Business Review*, 78(2), 67-75.

Daft, R. (1983), *Organization Theory and Design*, New York: West.

Dierickx, L. and Cool, K. (1989). Asset Stock Accumulation and Sustainability of Competitive Advantage, *Management Science*, 35, 1504-1511.

Dixon, N. (2000). *Common Knowledge: How Companies Thrive By Sharing What They Know*, Harvard University Press, Boston.

Eisenhardt, K. M., & Martin, J. A. (2000). Dynamic capabilities: what are they? *Strategic management journal*, 21(10-11), 1105-1121.

Grant, R.M. (1991). The Resource-Based Theory of Competitive Advantage: Implications for Strategy Formulation, *California Management, Review*, 33(1), 114-135.

Gregor, S. (2006). The nature of theory in information systems *MIS Quarterly*, 30(3), pp. 611-642.

Learned, E.P, Christensen, C.R., Andrews, K.R., and Guth, W. (1969). *Business Policy*, Homewood, IL: Irwin.

Levitt, B. and March, J. (1988). Organizational Learning, *Annual Review of Sociology*, 14, 319–340.

Nelson, R. and Winter, S. (1982). *An Evolutionary Theory of Economic Change* Cambridge, MA: Harvard University Press.

Okoli, C. and Mbarika, V.A.W. (2003). A Framework for Assessing E-Commerce in Sub-Saharan Africa, *Journal of Global Information Technology Management*, 6(3), 44-66.

Pavlou, P. A., & El Sawy, O. A. (2011). Understanding the elusive black box of dynamic capabilities. *Decision Sciences*, 42(1), 239-273.

Penrose, E.T. (1959). *The Theory of the Growth of the Firm*, New York: John Wiley and Sons.

Penrose, E.T. (1995). *The Theory of the Growth of the Firm*, 3rd Edition, Oxford: Oxford University Press.

Peteraf, M.A. (1993). The Cornerstone of Competitive Advantage: A Resource-Based View, *Strategic Management Journal*, 14(3), 179-191.

Porter, M.E. (1981). The Contributions of Industrial Organization to Strategic Management, *Academy of Management Review*, 6(4), 609-620.

Porter, M.E. (1990), *The Competitive Advantage of Nations*, London: Macmillan.

Prahalad, C.K., and Hamel, G. (1990). The Core Competence of the Corporation, *Harvard Business Review*, 68(3), 79-92.

Rindova, V. P., & Kotha, S. (2001). Continuous "morphing": Competing through dynamic capabilities, form, and function. *Academy of Management Journal*, 44(6), 1263-1280.

Rumelt, R. (1984). 'Towards a Strategic of the Firm'. In R. Lamb (ed) *Competitive Strategic Management*, Englewood Cliffs, NJ: Prentice-Hall, 556-570.

Sanchez, R., Heene, A. and Thomas, H. (1996). *Introduction: Towards the Theory and Practice of Competence-Based Competition*, Oxford: Pergamon Press.

Santhanam, R. and Hartono, E. (2003). Issues in Linking Information Technology Capability to Firm Performance, *MIS Quarterly*, 27(1), 125-153.

Schumpeter, J.A. (1934). *Theory of Economic Development*, Cambridge, MA: Harvard University Press.

Teece, D. J., Pisano, G. and Shuen, A. (1997). Dynamic capabilities and strategic management. *Strategic Management Journal*, 18(7), 509-533.

Teece, D.J. (1982). Towards an Economic Theory of the Multiproduct Firm, *Journal of Economic Behaviour and Organisation*, 3(1), 39-63.

Wade, M. & Hulland, J. (2004). Review: The resource-based view and information systems research: Review, extension and suggestions for future research. *MIS Quarterly*, 28(1), 107-142.

Wang, C.L. & Ahmed, P.K. (2007). Dynamic capabilities: a review and research agenda, *International Journal of Management Reviews*, 9(1), 31-51.

Wernerfelt, B. (1984). A Resource-Based View of the Firm, *Strategic Management Journal*, 5(2), 171-180.

Williamson, O. E. (1999). Strategy research: governance and competence perspectives.

Williamson, O.E. (1975). *Markets and Hierarchies*, New York: Free Press.

Williamson, O.E. (1985). *The Economic Institutions of Capitalism: Firms, Markets and Relational Contracting*, New York: Free Press.

Winter, S.G. (2000). The Satisfying Principle in Capability Learning", *Strategic Management Journal*, 21(10-11), 981-996.

Winter, S.G. (2003). Understanding Dynamic Capabilities", *Strategic Management Journal*, 24(10), 991-995.

Zikmund, W. G. (2003). *Business Research Methods*, 7th edition, Thomson/South-Western.

www.ingramcontent.com/pod-product-compliance
Lightning Source LLC
Chambersburg PA
CBHW071818200526
45169CB00018B/402